AF471084

LONG SHADOWS
CAST BEFORE

The engaging woodcut reproduced here as a frontispiece was specially drawn by George Cruikshank for Samuel Lewis's *Atlas [of] the Counties of Ireland*, published to accompany his *Topographical Dictionary* in 1837. It illustrates the spirit of national optimism abroad in the years half-way between Catholic emancipation and the Famine. A band of cheerful infants lay before a pretty young Erin (leaning her elbow negligently on her harp) a sheaf of corn, bolts of linen, a barrel (of stout?), fish, a palette, a brick, bales, an anchor, a wooden pail of milk. In the background, lighthouse, steam and sailing ships, factory chimneys, limekiln, and grazing cattle: the symbols of harmony and prosperity.

The map on page xiv is taken from the same source.

LONG SHADOWS CAST BEFORE

Nine Lives in Ulster, 1625–1977

C. E. B. BRETT

John Bartholomew & Son Limited
Edinburgh and London

British Library Cataloguing in Publication Data

Brett, Charles Edward Bainbridge
  Long shadows cast before.
  1. Brett family
  2. Northern Ireland — History
  I. Title
  929'. 2'09416   CS449.B/

  ISBN 0-7028-1058-4

First published in Great Britain 1978 by
JOHN BARTHOLOMEW & SON LIMITED
12 Duncan Street, Edinburgh EH9 1TA
and 216 High Street, Bromley BR1 1PW
© C. E. B. Brett, 1978

ISBN 0 7028 1058 4

Book and jacket design: Susan Waywell
11/12pt VIP Bembo

Printed in Great Britain by
Biddles Ltd, Guildford, Surrey.

For my grandchildren,
if and when,
and theirs.

CONTENTS

INTRODUCTION

E.M. Forster memorably described the poet Cavafy as 'standing absolutely motionless at a slight angle to the universe'. I, too, find myself at a slight angle to the universe; or perhaps the universe is at a slight angle to me. It is notorious that the Irish and Anglo-Irish of Ulster find themselves in a difficulty of identity. This book is an endeavour to locate myself, not only in space: where do I belong? how did I come to belong here? – but also in time: in the present, through my own experience: in history, through the experience of my family during the past 300 years.

It springs from a trenchant remark at the family dinner-table, when I gloomily doubted if any of my sons would choose to stay and make his home in Ulster; for the Troubles were dragging interminably on, no solution was in sight, many young people were emigrating. 'Nonsense' said my Aunt Chris sharply: 'this kind of thing has happened at least once in the lifetime of each generation of the family. One must just stay and make the best of it'.

It is true that few generations in Ulster have been fortunate enough to miss the cycle of rebellion, war, riot, and famine. The events of 1688, 1798, and 1886 are not much different in kind from those since 1968. I have thought it worth while to explore so much as I could of the history of each generation of my forebears, and (by way sometimes of reflection, sometimes of contrast) to explore the experiences of my own lifetime. This book therefore consists partly of Irish history, partly of family history, partly of recent events, partly of autobiography: but it is my hope to show that each casts light, if sometimes obliquely, on the others.

I hesitated before using family history in this way. Ancestor-worship is an unloveable foible. One's own family history is seldom of equal interest to other people. In the end I decided the risk was worth taking if only because, except for landed families, such accounts are extremely rare in Ireland. I have been exceptionally fortunate in having at my disposal letters and documents of every generation since the mid seventeenth century – though far fewer than a similar family in England might expect to have. Attainder, bankruptcy, bombing, an accidental fire, which burned the contents of my great-grandfather's study, the destruction of the public records of Ireland in the Four Courts: it is a wonder that any papers have survived at all.

A fair amount has been written about the aristocracy, the landed gentry, and the commercial and industrial dynasties of the British Isles. This is an account of a family that came, at best, of the very minor gentry; predominantly of professional men, lawyers for the most part, and clergymen, with a sprinkling of land agents and merchants; a family that attained modest prosperity from time to time, never substantial wealth or large estates; and that dipped once into bankruptcy. The lawyers in my family tree are as numerous as crabs on a crab-apple tree: and this too may make this book worth while: for if little has been written about the history of the legal profession in England, almost nothing has been written about it in Ireland.

The family has been in most generations rather untypical; there has been a radical and unconventional thread running through it; although firmly rooted in the Protestant tradition, my ancestors have been occasionally anti-clerical, and frequently anti-unionist. There has also been a cultural thread: a sustained interest in music, literature, the arts; and by contrast, the total absence of a sporting thread: no jolly hunting squarsons, no footballers, golfers, or bridge-fiends. The existence of this other, minority, tradition of liberal and cultivated enlightenment amongst the dour Protestants of Ulster has not received much attention.

I know that many of my opinions run counter to those of most of my fellow-Ulstermen. Probably a large majority will dissent, some very violently, from the views I express on past and on recent events. But I think they will mostly recognise without undue dismay that my attitudes slip, like jigsaw-puzzle pieces, into an understandable pattern against a known background. I hope I have sufficiently demonstrated, on the one hand, my right to speak as an Ulsterman whose roots go deep; on the other hand, enough experience of the world outside Ulster to speak with some impartiality and a measure of detachment. If this book is addressed first to my fellow-Ulstermen, it is addressed also to my fellow-countrymen throughout Ireland, and my fellow-citizens throughout Britain, both of whom have been puzzled and bewildered by the enigma of Ulster in recent years. If there are any who find that enigma less incomprehensible after reading this book, I shall be well content. But mostly this book is to the address of posterity: it contains no solutions to the problems of the present, only suggestions for possible lines to be pursued at some unknown date in the future. 'What has posterity ever done for us?' asked Sir Boyle Roche. For myself, it has given me hope; hope that some time in the future, if not yet, not now, a solution will be found to the troubles of the unhappy province that is my home.

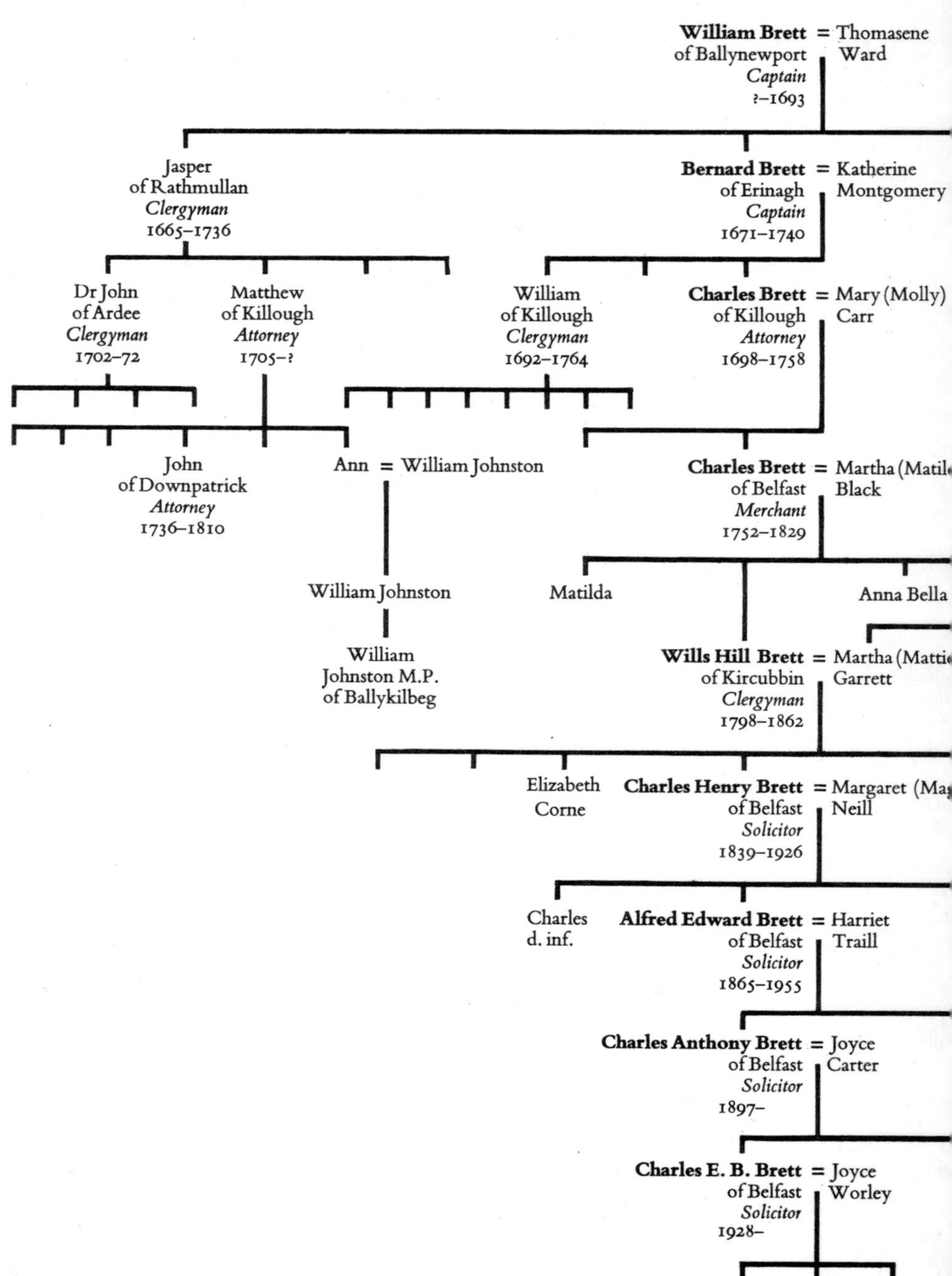

William Brett
of Ballynewport
Captain
?–1693
= Thomasene Ward

Jasper
of Rathmullan
Clergyman
1665–1736

Bernard Brett
of Erinagh
Captain
1671–1740
= Katherine Montgomery

Dr John
of Ardee
Clergyman
1702–72

Matthew
of Killough
Attorney
1705–?

William
of Killough
Clergyman
1692–1764

Charles Brett
of Killough
Attorney
1698–1758
= Mary (Molly) Carr

John
of Downpatrick
Attorney
1736–1810

Ann = William Johnston

Charles Brett
of Belfast
Merchant
1752–1829
= Martha (Matilda) Black

William Johnston

Matilda

Anna Bella

William
Johnston M.P.
of Ballykilbeg

Wills Hill Brett
of Kircubbin
Clergyman
1798–1862
= Martha (Mattie) Garrett

Elizabeth Corne

Charles Henry Brett
of Belfast
Solicitor
1839–1926
= Margaret (Maggie) Neill

Charles
d. inf.

Alfred Edward Brett
of Belfast
Solicitor
1865–1955
= Harriet Traill

Charles Anthony Brett
of Belfast
Solicitor
1897–
= Joyce Carter

Charles E. B. Brett
of Belfast
Solicitor
1928–
= Joyce Worley

THE BRETT FAMILY:
a selective genealogical tree

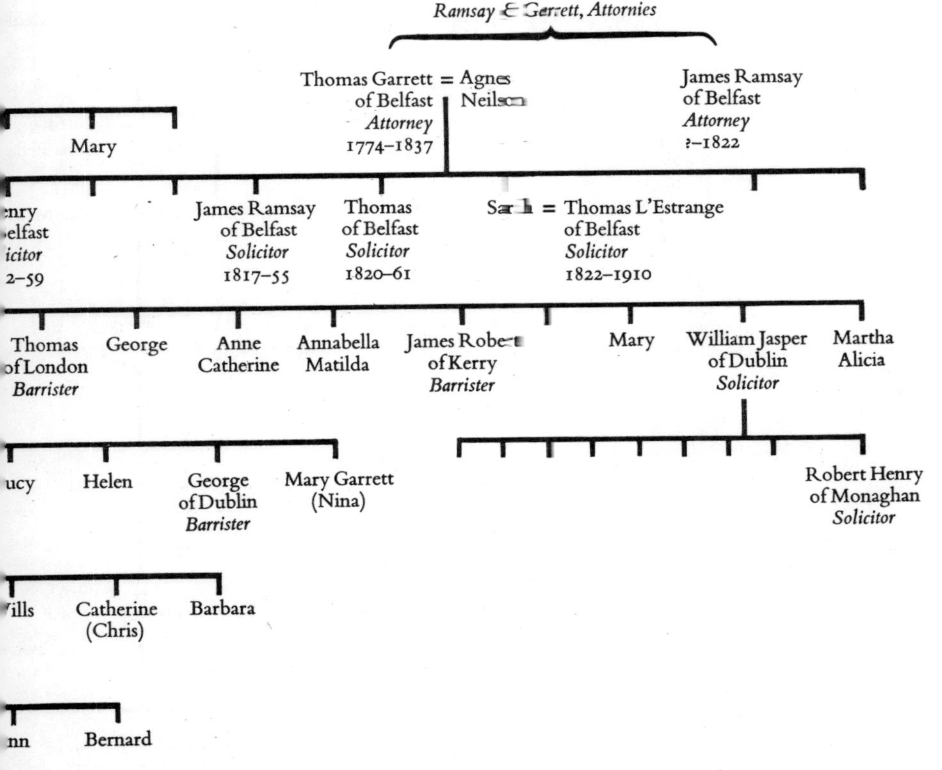

SCALE OF IRISH MILES

SCALE OF ENGLISH MILES

(From Samuel Lewis's *Atlas* [of] the Counties of Ireland.)

ONE

Of the people of the north-east counties of Ireland, some think of themselves as Irishmen; some think of themselves as British; some think of themselves as Ulstermen (whether belonging to the Ulster of nine counties, or the lesser Ulster of six counties) first and foremost.

Their relationships to each other, to their various traditions, to the strands of history, to the land itself, are complex and often contradictory. My own loyalties are strained and divided; but I start with one great advantage over most of my countrymen: I know with precision where, in space at any rate, my centre of gravity lies. Its latitude is 54° 35′ 49″ 68N.; its longitude is 05° 55′ 37″ 53W.; it is at a height of 29 feet above mean sea-level as defined by a mark near the base of Poolbeg lighthouse. That is the position of my chair in the office of the family firm: the chair in which my father, my grandfather, and my great-grandfather sat before me. It is a very ordinary mid-Victorian partner's swivelling-chair, the seat and half-moon of back and arms upholstered in scuffed crimson leather.

My room is high-ceilinged and well-proportioned; it was once the dining-room in a tall late-Georgian terrace house. Two houses survive out of the seven built in 1804; four storeys, attic, and basement, of brick, now a sooty mulberry colour; the doorways have Doric columns of sandstone, and cobweb fanlights; they and the Georgian glazing-bars in the large windows are painted ivory; the solid doors are painted dark blue; the door-knockers, black. Outside, the street is of tarmac, but it was not always so. When the firm moved in, my great-grandfather paid at his own expense for the repaving of the carriageway with wood blocks, instead of square-setts, to deaden the noise of the passing market carts and drays. The blocks were lifted during the last war, and my father claimed title to them: they provided us with the very best of firewood for several years thereafter.

The room is presently papered in a rather sombre pattern of red and gilt. It has two doors, and a very large three-light window, which formerly overlooked the basement courtyard, stables, and coach-house at the back. In its centre there stands a large mid-Victorian mahogany partner's desk, the top covered in dark-green leather, usually concealed by untidy piles of papers. The patterned Donegal carpet has several worn patches. The mantelpiece is of plain mahogany; the old-fashioned gas-fire is surrounded by William Morris pomegranate-pattern tiles. On the mantel-shelf stand: a French black marble striking clock; a brass candle-stick with snuffer; two rather fine ammonites; a dark-green bottle with a crown top, once holding smelling-salts, now containing only the ghost of an antique smell; and a modest flock of Rockingham and Staffordshire sheep and lambs, some several times repaired. There are also three painted porcelain flower-vases; but for most of the year, one of these will be standing on the desk, filled with flowers, usually roses: I bring a fresh bunch from my garden each Monday morning.

The recesses to left and right of the fireplace are filled to the ceiling by bookshelves: to the left, a set of the King's and Queen's Bench reports bound in brown cloth; to the right, the Chancery reports bound in green. Between the two hang the likenesses (silhouettes, a single daguerrotype, photographs) of all but one of the past partners in the firm; a striking photograph of a liner ablaze (M.V. *Bermuda,* in Belfast docks, 1931); and in the middle an oil painting by Colin Middleton called 'Sun and Moon', depicting an Egyptian queen walking a tightrope, with a blue-green background, which goes very well with the bindings of the Chancery reports. An English textile magnate once made me an offer of £20,000 for this painting, only to withdraw the offer a moment later on discovering that it was not by Klee.

The room contains also a mahogany standing desk, beside the window; a slim and handsome brass umbrella-stand in the Regency style; two built-in wall safes, papered over to match the rest of the walls; three late-Chippendale and four early-Victorian chairs, all of mahogany, all with seats upholstered in crimson leather, ranged around the walls against the chair-rail (there is no picture-rail); and a very large and peculiar Victorian chair, now used by clients, by the fire-side. The back of this only is upholstered in leather, but the seat is of polished mahogany, very crisply hollowed out to accommodate each buttock separately. It was specially constructed to meet the needs of my greatgrandfather, who in his latter years was a martyr both to constipation and to piles.

Against the wall behind my chair stands an enormous, and very fine, mahogany breakfront book-case, the sections divided by pilasters with palmetto capitals. It formerly belonged to John Rea, a slightly deranged Orange Nationalist solicitor, who spent much of his working life sueing the Unionist mayor and aldermen of Belfast for exceeding their powers; in this he was successful, having them personally sur-charged with a sum of £83,000. This happy association gives me constant pleasure. The bottom half contains cupboards; these are for putting things in, not for taking things out. I have at various times found in them mid-nineteenth-century blue books, an annotated copy of the Treaty of Versailles, and my father's gas-mask, issued in 1938, in its original canvas carrier.

On the lowest book-shelf is a battered set of all the statutes passed by the Parliament of Ireland in twenty-one large volumes, bound in musty brown leather with gilt tooling. This is more for show than for everyday use. The earliest Act is one passed in 1310, under Edward II, by the Parliament of Kilkenny; 'An Act to restrain great Lords from taking up lodging or sojourning against the will of the owner': it provides that such manner of destructions shall be holden for open robbery; squatters, noble or ignoble, still pose a problem in Ireland today. Half-way through the last volume is to be found the Act of Union, providing that 'the kingdoms of Great Britain and Ireland shall, upon the first day of January, 1801, *and for ever,* be united into one kingdom'. (As my father taught me when I was his apprentice, *for ever* is a long time, and the words should be used sparingly.) The last statute of the Irish Parliament, cap. 100 of 40 Geo III, was an Act for the better regulation of the butter trade, and also respecting sedan chairs, coaches, and chaises plying for hire, within the city and liberties of Cork.

On the shelf above, for daily use rather than for show, stand the statutes of the Parliament of Northern Ireland from 1921 to 1972. The first statute was a single-clause Act empowering the infant Ministry of Finance to borrow a sum not exceeding £160,000; the last was the Agriculture (Abolition of County Committees) Act (Northern Ireland) 1972. Since that date, the Orders in Council of direct rule have been published in volumes, of which one is optimistically entitled, on the spine, 'Northern Ireland Statutes Etc': I think this elegant choice of words must be the binder's.

Beside and above the statutes are the numerous standard text-books needed for day-to-day life, side by side with directories (some ancient, some modern), dictionaries, maps and guides, Fowler's *English Usage,* the Treaty of Rome, a few volumes of poetry (great-grandfather's), a few volumes on architecture (mine), and a great number of dusty and obsolete law-books ranging from the *Young Clerk's Vademecum,* Belfast, 1754, to the works of great-great-uncle Thomas Brett, barrister, of London.

The room contains, of course, many other articles, the accretions of several generations. There is a telephone; close by, the four nicely carved mouth-pieces of an ingenious speaking-tube system installed in the 1880s, each mouthpiece having a carved whistle on a chain with which to attract the attention of the person at the other end. There is a box of quill pens, and a supply of ink cartridges for my own Parker pen. Drawers and cupboards are full of surprises as well as dust. On the walls, there are three early views of Belfast, one showing the office soon after it was built. There is a framed letter of 1865 from great-grandfather to a rival solicitor he did not like, of exemplary crispness: it reads, in its entirety: 'Dear Sir: Thompson with Anketell: Quod obstet?: truly yours: [signed with a flourish]'. And there is a woodcut poster advertising the display of a mammoth's skeleton in the Belfast Assembly Rooms about 1830.

I have left till last the parchment, mounted on red linen in a large scarred gilt frame, that hangs on the wall opposite the window. At the top is a portrait woodcut of King Charles the Second, framed in arabesques, curlicues, roses, tulips, pinks, an ear of wheat, heraldic beasts, a butterfly, and a dragonfly. At the foot, still attached by its original ribbon, appends a disc of brown wax — large as a saucer — bearing the impress of the Great Seal of Ireland. This is the original grant of Letters Patent, dated 29 October 1684, over some 400 acres of land in County Down to my great-great-great-great-great-great-grandfather,* William Brett.

* In the words that Sir Walter Scott, with gentle mockery, puts into the mouth of his Antiquary, referring to his great-great-great-grandfather — 'it's a shame to the English language that we have not a less clumsy way of expressing a relationship of which we have occasion to think and speak so frequently'!

TWO

I do not know when or where William Brett was born. I do not even know for sure whether he was Irish or English. The name 'Brett' is usually taken to mean Breton, not British, so one way or the other the origin of the family goes back to the followers of the Norman King William, themselves only a few generations descended from Viking marauders. He may have been related to the Bretts of Tulloke, County Meath, a family descended from the 'old English' or Anglo-Norman settlers in Ireland of the twelfth and thirteenth centuries. According to a copy of a fragmentary family tree, said to have been taken from the College of Arms in 1755, he was son of Jasper Brett of Bricklew, County Sligo, who was son of John de Brytte of Tulloke. It is quite likely; the family arms and motto are almost the same. Or, he may have been related to a Lieutenant Jerome Brett who played an active part in Sir Thomas Smith's expedition of 1572 to colonise the Ards peninsula of County Down. (Indeed, Jerome may have been one of the Bretts of Tulloke himself.) Or he may simply have been an English adventurer: my great-grandfather thought he might have been a younger son of a family of Bretts from Kent. Whatever his origins, he was a professional soldier, and a Protestant. None of his letters survive; all I know is derived from copies of a few deeds, and of his will; and passing references in contemporary documents.

His name first appears in 1625, in a list of nine lieutenants who had served in the Palatinate, in the early stages of the Thirty Years' War, short-listed, out of an earlier list of forty-seven names, for service in Ireland as captains. The recommendation came from no less a sponsor than the Prince (or Elector) of Bohemia, father of Prince Rupert of the Rhine. This was Sir Horace Vere's expedition, an unofficial venture, which set out in 1620, with the approval, but not the financial support, of James I. 'The young nobility so strong for officers' places that the experienced officers are thrown out', says a letter of 14 July 1620; by the following year the expeditionary force, far smaller than had been intended, was already in difficulties. General Vere is in great straits, but hopes to be relieved by the King of Denmark; his men are four months' pay in arrear'. In February 1623 Sir Horace had returned, his tail somewhat between his legs.

No doubt young William Brett (probably aged no more than sixteen) learned how to live without pay — a very necessary lesson at this period. There was nothing exotic or unusual about foreign adventures such as this; the younger sons of many English, Irish, and Scottish families undertook military service abroad; two of the Stewart brothers of Castlestewart served in Swedish regiments of mercenaries under Count Mansfeld at this period. William Brett seems to have served in Ireland as a captain, without promotion, for over forty years. This period of service was exceptionally arduous; it included the great rising of 1641; the laborious campaigns that followed it, complicated by the Civil War in England; Cromwell's Irish campaign of 1649 to 1650; and the long-drawn-out years of policing and consolidation that followed. Where my forebear's loyalties lay, as between cavaliers and roundheads (to express it in very English terms), I have been unable, from the scanty evidence available, to deduce.

This was one of the most wretched periods of Irish history, for civilians certainly, for soldiers also. There was cruelty and savagery on both sides; there was starvation, disease, and desolation throughout the countryside. In 1642 the army was very close to mutiny; in July the Lords Justice in Dublin wrote desperately to London,

> above all we must still call upon your lordships for supply of treasure . . . for all borrowings here are long since at an end, and no way left unattempted to keep the army from disbanding. . . . Not only the common soldier (whose necessities were in some degree hitherto supplied by pillage, whilst there was any pillage to be had) but also the officers (. . . whose sufferings and provocations for want of pay have been also greater than the common soldiers, selling by degrees all their clothes and all they have to keep them alive) are all at last reduced to such lamentable extremities as is a grief and shame to behold.

Although (from the army's point of view) things improved after Cromwell's arrival, they never reached the point where any officer or soldier could expect to receive his pay in full.

In theory, the pay of a captain of foot in 1660 was £11 4s. a month — private soldiers received 14 shillings a month. In practice, any serving soldier might count himself lucky to receive two thirds of his pay, and that usually several years in arrear. In the early 1660s William Brett was stationed with Sir Robert Hannay's company of foot at Bellahy, 'a strong regular fort, lately built with bulwarks of lime and stone, on a considerable pass between the counties of Mayo and Sligo'. He had under him an ensign, a sergeant, a drummer, and twenty privates; in 1662 he received a sum of £338 14s. 10d. in part payment of an amount of £498 13s. 6d. due to himself and the men under him for the period, long since elapsed, from August 1658 to February 1660. At some time during this period he married Thomasene Ward, the daughter of a fellow-officer from County Down; their eldest son, Jasper, was born in Fermanagh in 1665. At last, in 1657, he received a grant of lands in settlement of the arrears of pay of some forty-odd years; and was able to take his retirement.

But, like many another, William Brett found himself caught up in the intricacies of the new land settlement. For twenty-five years past, all that was done in Ireland had been financed on the assumption that the winners should be paid in land out of the spoils of victory. There were four difficulties about this in practice. First, that of establishing whose land should be forfeited: it was not the intention of Parliament 'to extirpate the whole nation', and a sliding scale was proposed under which the landowners of 1641 were to forfeit one fifth, one third, or two thirds of their lands, according to the degree of their complicity in the rising; with the penalties of death and total forfeiture at one extreme for the leaders, total exemption from forfeiture at the other extreme for those who had 'manifested their constant good affection to the commonwealth of England'. This difficulty was vastly increased after the restoration when many royalist landowners appealed to a not unsympathetic Charles II for the return of their lands.

Second, there was the difficulty of determining who should be allocated the lands so made available. The principal categories of claimants were the '49 Officers, so called – that is, officers who had served in Ireland before 5 June 1649, and were owed large arrears of pay; of these William Brett was one – and the Adventurers: those English merchants who had advanced money to the Government on the security of debentures promising them payment, after the war, in confiscated land. Many of these obligations had been entered into over twenty years earlier: debentures had changed hands; impecunious soldiers had pledged or sold their rights; and a whole new category of unprincipled speculators now came forward to claim a share.

Third, there was no satisfactory system for determining who was to have which land, and no accurate method of assessing the comparative values of good arable soil on the one hand, and the bog, moorland, and mountainside (comprising so much of Ireland) on the other. This was very material, since the scheme propounded by Cromwell involved the removal of the former owners from the comparatively prosperous eastern counties, and the allocation to them instead of acres in the wilder territories of Connaught.

Finally, there simply was not enough forfeited land to go round amongst the claimants.

Books of Survey and Distribution were ultimately prepared, showing the address of each holding by county, barony, parish, and townland; the name of the proprietor in 1641; the number of acres respectively profitable and unprofitable in each plot; the person to whom it was aplotted; and the rent that he was thenceforward to pay to the Crown. An undated volume, perhaps as late as 1680, survives in the Public Record Office of Northern Ireland. According to this, very substantial acreages were aplotted to William Brett: not only lands in the north-east, but also 573 acres of profitable land at Ballybeggan, Co. Kerry — previously owned by one Walter Hussey. 'The castle of Ballybeggan, formerly a place of considerable strength belonging to the Desmonds, and a noted pass between Tralee and Castle Island, was the only fortress in the county that in 1641 held out against the Irish forces, and it resisted every assault until relieved in 1643, by Lord Inchiquin's forces: during the war of the Revolution it was burned by the Irish'. But of this Kerry estate no more is heard amongst the family records; it was probably sold at an early date so that William Brett could consolidate his estates in County Down, close to the home of his in-laws, the Wards, near Strangford in Lecale.

According to the same Book of Survey, William Brett was granted (in a few instances jointly with others) almost 1,150 acres in Lecale. But there are many puzzling features about these grants. More than half of this acreage is stated to have belonged to Protestants in good standing in 1641. Some of the lands had previously belonged to a Protestant family named Fitz Symons; some of the lands (not always the same) were regranted to William Brett jointly with Nicholas Fitz Symons. The lands of Ballystrew, formerly the property of Patrick Russell, were allotted to William Brett; but 'Patrick's widow having travelled on foot to London from Holyhead (not having means to proceed by the public vehicle) Charles II, at her earnest remonstrance and petition, had these grants abrogated, whereupon the lands were returned to Patrick (her son) by the Court of Grace'. Only 49 acres at Myra, formerly the property of one Shane Tumelty, and perhaps 69 acres at Ballyregan, formerly the property of one Christopher Welsh, look at all like confiscated lands. And indeed, there are evidences of earlier purchases, sales, leases, and releases in Lecale involving William Brett dating from 1667, 1668, 1670, 1673, and 1677, though none of these deeds has survived. It looks as though the Book of Survey and Distribution involved a fair amount of wishful thinking; not all turned out on the ground as its draftsmen had intended; many plots of land had evidently already been the subject-matter of transactions of which they were unaware; and there may have been horse-trading amongst the new grantees. Something under half the land in the barony of Lecale was intended to be redistributed amongst fifteen owners: of these, the Duke of York and the Earl of Kildare were absentees: the Cromwell family (no relation) received substantial grants in the vicinity of Ardglass: the Wards were granted lands at Castleward, which they had already owned anyway for more than a century: the Bishop of Dromore was to receive substantial endowments, but these included a whole townland already bought, paid for, and occupied by William Brett. The remaining grantees – Brett, Everard, Hammond, West, Gibbons, Audley, Fitz Symons, Lindsay, and Hamilton – received their lands in the form of widely scattered plots, not consolidated holdings. Of the eight townlands in which William Brett was granted land, four were on the northern shore, between Strangford and the River Quoile; two were on the southern shore, between St John's Point and Tyrella; two lay inland on the road from Tyrella to Downpatrick. From the point of view of practical farming, this must have been an impossible situation. Was it a deliberate act of policy on the part of Government to prevent the old soldiers from becoming too powerful and prosperous? It is perhaps not mere coincidence that only the large and unified holding of the Ward family survived without change of ownership into the nineteenth century.

The generally confused state of affairs, which had been getting worse ever since the 1650s, was resolved (more or less) by the appointment of a new body of Commissioners in March 1684. Although their function was partly to raise new funds, they were directed to take note of the fact that some of the Patents previously granted 'have been found to be void, insufficient in law, defective, imperfect, voidable, defeasible, or so obscure that much trouble and disquiet may arise in proof of title'. The parchment that hangs on my wall was prepared on the orders of these Commissioners; the lands granted by them to William Brett (all of which he already occupied) were considerably more modest than those allotted to him in the Book of Survey and Distribution. On the northern coast of Lecale, he was granted Walshestown Castle and some 225 acres; eight miles to the south-west, he was granted some 164 acres at Ballynewport: he had already purchased the townland of Ringbane, close to Walshestown, and the townland of Ballydonnell, close to Ballynewport, and retained them until his death, although they are not mentioned in the Letters Patent.

He had chosen to make his home, rather surprisingly, on the smaller farm. Ballynewport house was 'a long low rambling mansion with dormer windows'; close to it was a rath or fort, with a spring of fresh water, later converted by his son Jasper into a convenient fish-pond. House and rath alike have long since disappeared: indeed, both had already disappeared when the first ordnance survey was made in the 1830s. Today there are only a handful of small farms scattered in the rushy and rather melancholy valley, closed in by low rocky hills so that the sea, less than a couple of miles away, is invisible. By contrast, Walshestown is on a most attractive site: the tall square stone four-storey tower-house, probably built in the late sixteenth century and still in excellent order, stands by a stream in a sheltered and wooded valley, looking out over the quiet waters of Strangford Lough and the estuary of the Quoile. Perhaps the castle was already tenanted, for the Anderson family lived in it till the mid nineteenth century, and claimed then to have lived in it since the reign of Charles I. Or perhaps William Brett did not care to live so very close to his in-laws, the Wards, whose lands of Castleward marched with his of Walshestown.

From 1667 until its forced sale by the next generation, Ballynewport was the family home. (One relic of that period, still in the family, a tall cane-backed armchair of carved oak, of around 1660, may have come from that house-furnishing.) Here William Brett's two younger sons and daughter were born. Here he settled down as a respected country gentleman. He was on friendly terms with the Cromwells. Edward, third baron Cromwell, had been appointed Governor of Lecale in 1605, having purchased a great part of Phelim MacCartan's territory in County Down; his son, an officer in the Royalist army, became Viscount Lecale and later Earl of Ardglass. The fourth, and last, Earl and Countess were close family friends, as well as near neighbours, whom he advised about complex legal proceedings: in 1682, 'Mr. Brett's letter tells me a hellish story': it almost looks as though he was not merely a man of affairs, but himself actually a lawyer. He undertook the kind of duties in the county to be expected of a retired military man: in 1678 he was High Sheriff; in the same year he was appointed one of three local gentry to accept surrenders of arms when an Order in Council prohibited persons of the Popish religion from presuming to 'ride with, carry, buy, use or keep any halberts, pikes, muskets, calivers, fowling-pieces, carbines, pistols or other guns whatsoever without licence'. What echoes the words arouse, exactly three centuries later! And six years later, Captain Brett was deputed to take the evidence of Alexander Finiston of Downpatrick, 'charged, out of his own mouth, with being active in a design, which the Presbyterians are said to have, of rising up in arms, and with being a rider up and down the country to give notice of the time . . . one damnable conspiracy': but unfortunately his examination of the witness was not considered sufficiently searching by the Duke of Ormonde, who demanded that Finiston be sent to Dublin.

William Brett was by now an old man, but the easy country life of his retirement was overtaken by disaster. In November 1688 William III landed at Torbay. Ireland was under the control of Lord Tyrconnell; the Catholic party was rallying to the support of James II; in December 1688 her agent wrote to the widowed Lady Ardglass in London: 'since the late news of wars in England, within this fortnight the English and Scotch are under such apprehension of fear that the Irish will rise and kill and rob them, that several families are gone out of Lecale and this town'. And a week later, 'Mr Brett and his wife give your ladyship their hearty thanks for your kind offer' of a passage in a ship from Ardglass harbour. That offer was almost certainly accepted, then or soon afterwards. On 12 March King James landed in Ireland. Two days later occurred the battle known as 'the break of Dromore', a mere twenty miles from Ballynewport, which opened all the north (save the fortified towns of Derry and Enniskillen) to Tyrconnell's troops. Every Protestant who could do so fled to England, Kintyre, Wigtown, or the Isle of Man. Two months later the 'Patriot Parliament' sitting in Dublin passed an Act of Attainder declaring traitors, if they should fail to acknowledge the sovereignty of King James, 2,461 named Irish Protestants, condemning them to death, and to forfeiture of their entire estates and property. They included William Brett; his eldest son, Jasper, then aged twenty-three and an undergraduate at Trinity College, Dublin; and his second son, Bernard, then aged eighteen. The list 'of Protestants of Ireland lately fled out of the Kingdom for the safety of their lives' gives also 'the yearly value of their estates, now either sequestered by the Papists, or so kept from them that they neither do nor can receive profit of them'. The Brett properties are shown as having an annual value of £160; a surprisingly low figure compared to a captain's pay, twenty-five years earlier, of £135 per annum.

No family letters or records of this period survive; I do not know where the Bretts fled, nor when they returned, nor in what state they found their home. I wish I did. By the end of the summer the siege of Derry had failed, General Schomberg had arrived with reinforcements at Carrickfergus, and the Ulster counties were lost to King James. The Battle of the Boyne was fought on 1 July (old style) in the following year; and William Brett was certainly home again by 23 September 1690, when he made his will. He starts by declaring himself to be 'in perfect health and of good and sound memory, praise be to Almighty God'. He leaves Ballynewport house and lands to his wife for life, together with 'all my plate and household stuff . . . as also all my stock of black cattle and sheep and garrans (which are now but small)' — garrans are rough Irish ponies; was it they, or the stock, that was small? — 'and all the graine which I shall then have in and above ground'. He leaves Jasper all the lands, entailed to his children and grandchildren; to Bernard '20 pounds a year to be paid to him during such time as he shall remain undisposed of or unmarried till he shall attain the age of 21 years', and 'after he shall think fit to dispose of himself in marriage or betake himself to any other course of life', £200 instead; a marriage portion of £400 'to my dearly beloved daughter Mary'; £20 to a favourite niece, and £10 to the poor of the parish; and he gives instructions regarding a debt of £250 due to Mr John Griffith of Comber, secured on mortgages of 1683 and 1684, and directs that 'all other my debts which I shall owe at the date of my death' are to be coped with 'as learned Counsel in the law shall reasonably advise'; and he provides what is to happen 'in case any creditor shall be so impatient as not to expect satisfaction for his debt according to the provision herein made'.

These debts were to loom large in the life of the next generation. It is likely that William Brett's finances were dealt a damaging blow, to put it no higher, by the sequestration of his estates in 1689. But there may have been another cause for the embarrassment of his finances. According to family tradition, William Brett spent too many of his evenings playing at cards with his in-laws and neighbours, the Wards of Castle-ward; and was obliged to raise substantial sums on the property to meet his card debts. Perhaps the fact that they had won so much money from the Bretts accounts for the generosity with which the Wards treated his impecunious descendants. So my great-grandfather hinted to my father, many years ago. Certain it is that when William died in 1693 his debts were numerous and heavy.

THREE

The year 1620, when William Brett set off eastwards to seek adventure in the Palatinate, was the year also when the *Mayflower* made her westward landfall at Cape Cod. The settlement of planters in Ireland was almost simultaneous with the settlement of planters in North America. In 1629, soon after William Brett's return for service in Ireland, Charles I made grants of lands in Carolina and in Massachusetts Bay. John Endicott, recipient of the latter charter, with his own hands 'cut the cross from English flags on ships in Boston harbour lest this symbol be construed as popish' (an idea that seems not to have occurred to Dr Paisley). The charter for Maryland follwed in 1630; Connecticut in 1662; Pennsylvania in 1681.

There are many intriguing cross-references between the Irish and the American settlements. So early as 1606 Bacon thought the plantation of Ulster much more promising than that of Virginia. George Calvert, Baron Baltimore in the Irish peerage and a Catholic, sought to establish Maryland as a colony dedicated to religious tolerance. Colonel Robert Venables, who besieged and took Belfast for Oliver Cromwell in 1649, assisted William Penn six years later in the capture of Jamaica. The most interesting comparison, however, is that between the fate of the native Irish and the native Indians. The Irish were expelled from the richer lands of the eastern seaboard to the wilds of Connaught; the Indians were expelled to the wilds of the American interior. The Irish rising of 1641, followed by the Cromwellian wars, had their parallels in the massacres of Indians, and the retaliatory massacres by Indians, which took place in 1622, 1637, 1644, and 1676. Raiding and skirmishing continued in both countries until the end of the century.

There were differences, however, between the attitudes of the settlers to the heathen Red Indians and the Irish, who were, if papists, at least Christians of a kind. In New England 'opinion varied as to whether the Indians were children of the devil who might be exterminated and their lands appropriated, or whether they were heathen waiting for salvation who might profitably give up their lands in exchange for a celestial heritage'. As an independent people, the Indians were driven ever further into the wilderness, and ultimately exterminated by the Hotchkiss guns at Wounded Knee in 1890. It was never the policy of any English government to exterminate the native Irish: its object was rather to pacify and civilise the wild tribesmen, and assimilate them into the 'civil polity' of British society as it was then understood. Had it not been for the difference in religion between Protestant settlers and Catholic natives, this policy might have enjoyed more success than it did.

There survives to this day a certain identification between the more extreme Irish nationalists and the Red Indians. The Catholic farmer, looking down from his scraggy mountainside at the rich valley land below occupied by prosperous Protestant families, has something in common with the Indian brave looking down from a spur of the Black Hills of Dakota on the rolling prairies. The English soldier speaks of the wild country of South Armagh as 'Indian territory'; his stronghold in the Falls Road of Belfast is known as 'Fort Laramie'. Some, at least, of the Republican paramilitaries see themselves as the descendants of the native Irish who were expelled to Hell or Connaught, and the Protestants of twentieth-century Ulster as the heirs of the settlers by whom they were expelled. They ignore the fact that the native Irish themselves were the descendants of numerous earlier waves of invaders; they ignore the effects of three centuries of marriage and extra-marital social intercourse. They forget that each one of us possesses a total of 3,070 ancestors if he goes back nine generations; there can be no such thing as pure and unmixed racial descent, and if there were, it would be nothing to be proud of. They forget that, as Dr A. T. Q. Stewart has pointed out, 'many of the I.R.A. have planter surnames, and are probably of planter descent, while an Orangeman may be descended from Gaelic Kings'. They forget that there are more Irishmen in America than there are in Ireland, all more or less comfortably settled on land stolen from the Red Indians.

If there is something in common between militant republicans and the Red Indian tradition, there remains equally something in common between militant Protestants and the waggon-train settlers of the middle west. The spirit of the frontier has never quite died out in Ulster; and by the frontier, I do not mean the border; I mean a world of violence and surprise.

*   *   *   *

On the evening of 28 May 1972 my wife and I dined with friends near the south shore of Belfast Lough, some seven miles from the centre of the city. Sound travels far over water; as we were sitting talking after dinner, we heard a series of heavy explosions — nothing unusual about that, of course, in 1972 or since. Wryly I remarked that somebody was getting a battering tonight, and the conversation continued. We reached home about midnight. Soon afterwards, the telephone rang; it was one of my partners; 'You've heard by now, I suppose?' 'No, what?' 'The office has been blown up'. There was nothing more to be done that night, except to awaken our architect and arrange to meet him there at first light to assess the damage.

A stolen car, with an extremely large bomb in it, had been left in the narrow lane behind our office. No warning was given. It blew up (to quote the police report) 'at 8.56 p.m.', causing 'extensive damage over a wide area', and 'extensive structural damage to property near the seat of the explosion'. The lane is like a canyon, closely hemmed in by buildings on both sides, which magnified the effects of the blast. Our poor caretaker was blown right across his basement kitchen, but was fortunate enough to escape worse injury than shock, scratches, and bruises. I have no reason to think that the bomb was particularly aimed at us; the firm employed Catholics and Protestants with impartiality; many neighbours suffered equally; it was simply a place to achieve the maximum damage with the greatest economy of means.

Next morning was Bank Holiday Monday. It was a heart-breaking day, though it closed with the comforting advice that the main part of the building, farthest from the bomb, was not so unsafe that it must be demolished. My own room had come off comparatively lightly, shielded in part by the stable-block at the rear. Of course the window had been blown in, and sharp fragments of glass had scarred the furniture and walls; the door had been blown off its hinges. The damage was much worse upstairs. All the back windows, and their slim Georgian astragals, had been blown in; most of the panes at the front had been blown out; internal doors and partitions had been wrenched from the main walls; one of the two great beams carrying the roof had cracked and sagged; many slates were off; chunks of plaster had fallen from the ceilings: the whole building had been lifted a few inches into the air and then dropped again a fraction out of true; the staircase and the polished mahogany banister-rail were sadly scarred and battered; files, documents, papers, had been thrown into confusion; dislodged dirt and fragments of glass had been scattered everywhere.

The former stable-block at the rear took the full force of the blast. The car-bomb had been placed some eighteen inches from the outer wall of the strong-room; which, designed to resist fire, did not prove strong enough to resist fifty pounds of high explosives. The whole wall was blown in: one of the wheels of the car was found, a week later, blown some fifteen feet into the wreckage. The concrete slabs of the ceiling were canted crazily, many now resting only on the buckled remains of the steel shelving with which the strong-room had been lined. The rooms above were, of course, completely destroyed. Beyond the strong-room, a little further from the bomb, was the ground-floor office used by my father since his semi-retirement. That morning, the back wall to the lane had wholly disappeared, leaving the ceiling unsupported; but to my astonishment, the inlaid eighteenth-century grandfather clock, though scarred by glass, was still ticking, and showing the correct time. Alas, I made an incautious movement in the doorway: at 9.30 a.m. precisely the ceiling collapsed in front of me, and the poor clock disintegrated into hundreds of fragments under a pile of chalk and laths. (The pieces were collected, reassembled, and the clock painstakingly restored: it now keeps perfect time once again.)

It took a week before we knew how much, or little, had been lost. The beams of the strong-room ceiling had to be shored up individually, and the steel shelving (which had saved us from fire) laboriously cut away, section by section, with hammer and cold chisel. Within the pigeon-holes, deeds and documents had been compressed together like fish fingers as the shelving was hurled across the room; japanned tin deed-boxes had been twisted and crumpled; some bundles of papers were damaged by the rain that drove into the wreckage during that unhappy week: but only a few of the precious documents were lost or destroyed. Teams of us worked in our oldest clothes, filthy and often bleeding from scratches made by slivers of broken glass, to clear up the mess; to sort and label the papers; and to pack them into tea-chests for transport to the basement vaults of a neighbouring insurance company.

It took three years to settle our claim for compensation: since the building was an old one, the amount of the eventual award fell far short of the cost of replacing old with new.

It took almost five years to complete the rebuilding. We are now nearly, though not quite, back to normal. Some changes were unavoidable. There is no resident caretaker now: today I have a gas fire in my room instead of the fire of coal and turf that used to be laid and lit each morning in winter until 1972.

On the first working day after the explosion, I took a break for lunch, dirty and angry and dressed in my old clothes; at the table I met a Belfast business-man, a prominent Unionist and an Orangeman. I have never forgotten, and am unlikely ever to forgive, his first words to me: 'Well, sorry about your bomb, but it serves you right for your years in the Labour party'.

*   *   *   *

On the evening of 13 June 1974 I arrived home from work as usual around six o'clock. 'Home' was a comfortable foursquare former manse in the Malone Road area of Belfast. It was a very pleasant summer evening; the long avenue of lime trees was in full leaf. The children were away. My wife was waiting for me with the news: 'They say there's a car-bomb in the park behind us'. This was the parallel avenue some 75 yards away. Somebody had shouted a warning over the hedge; the ends of the avenue had been sealed off by the police, and the houses fronting it cleared. There had recently been a good many bombs in the city, mostly in commercial buildings, but there had also been a vast number of hoaxes and scares. 'I don't believe it' I said; 'let's sit down and have a glass of sherry. But we'd better keep away from the windows'. (There is always a quandary in a bomb-scare: if windows and doors are opened, the damage is minimised, for the blast-wave can travel freely till it spends itself: but anyone in the process of opening windows when the explosion comes may be dreadfully mutilated by flying glass.) We decided to leave the windows alone, poured ourselves sherry, and sat down in our usual chairs on either side of the fireplace in the sunny drawing-room.

Five minutes later, as we were sitting peaceably chatting and sipping, there was the loudest explosion I have (yet) heard; a sucking wave of blast; and all the glass in every window in the room fell shimmering and tinkling to the ground. By good fortune, it was the secondary inward wave, not the initial outward blast, that broke the windows; so that most of the fragments fell harmlessly onto the window-sill or into the rose-bed outside.

When we had collected ourselves – it took a little time – we went outside and joined our neighbours on their lawn; the police were afraid there might be another bomb, and had ordered everybody out of doors. We lay on the grass for three quarters of an hour before the all-clear was given. Then we dispersed to assess the damage. We were lucky. We had lost many window-panes; several doors and door-frames had been broken or displaced; a ceiling was cracked; a great many slates (as we were to discover next winter) had come loose. Our next-door neighbours had fared much worse: their roofs and ceilings were severely damaged. The house in the avenue behind us, outside which the car had been left, was almost completely destroyed: the owners (friends of ours) lost nearly everything they possessed.

That summer, each time I mowed my lawn, the blades of the motor mower would give a crunch and a shower of sparks when they struck some brown and mangled piece of metal hidden in the grass; these were fragments of the car that had been blown up.

*　　*　　*　　*

I do not recount these experiences because they are other than commonplace. Few people in Ulster since 1969 can have escaped happenings of this kind. Very many people suffered far more and far worse. Friends, colleagues, or acquaintances have had their homes or businesses burnt out, or totally destroyed; have been shot or shot at; one died of burns received when the bus she was travelling on was set on fire; one was murdered when he opened the door, as he thought, to the postman, while cooking the family breakfast; another was killed outright by bomb-blast. None of these things has – yet – happened to me, or to any close friend or near relation.

The most frightening thing is the extent to which one becomes hardened. This is neither insensitivity nor cynicism; it is a necessary mechanism of self-defence. In the first year of the Troubles, one listened intently to every news bulletin, and to the broadcasts of the Orange and Republican free-lance radio stations. One's heart turned over at the account of each new horror. One rushed to look at each new wall-poster – some of them, derived from the Paris student uprisings of 1968, were brilliant – I have still an illicitly obtained copy of the poster that read 'Malone Road fiddles while Falls Road burns'. One stood in the garden on summer evenings listening to fusillades of shots a mere mile away, wondering whose bullet had found what billet this time; watching the palls of smoke and sometimes the glare of flames from burning buildings, and wondering whose; listening to the windows rattle at the sound of unidentifiable explosions.

But after a year, still more after eight years, one no longer responds in the same way. The extraordinary has come, inevitably, to seem almost ordinary. When the morning news bulletin reports no bombs, no fires, no murders, no riots, no hijackings, then it has been a quiet night, and it is that that seems extraordinary (and in a depressing way, a little flat). The illegal radio stations have long since closed down: no more Free Belfast, no more Orange Lily at the record turntable. Such posters as now appear, and they are few, are dreary and uninteresting. Even the graffiti are uninspired, and rarely raise even a tired smile: as did the sudden rash of 'F.T.P.', which appeared all over the Protestant districts in 1970. (As Lord Hailsham remarked at the time, to Fuck the Pope remains an anatomical impossibility.) Today, when there is a bomb alarm, one evacuates briskly but with resignation, and tries to get on with one's work elsewhere till it is over. There is a traffic bollard near the City Hall that has often served me for an open-air desk. When there comes the crump of an explosion – unless it is very close – one perhaps looks at one's watch, so as to find out later which particular bang that had been; but work is not interrupted for more than a moment or two. And one comes almost to ignore the sinister bells and sirens, heard many times on most working days, which indicate that police cars, ambulances, fire engines, and the armoured cars of the bomb squad are galloping to an alarm.

As I have said, this is a necessary mechanism of self-defence: the protective scab that grows over even a deep wound. But I acknowledge, with distress, that it is inevitably accompanied by a coarsening of sensibility; a lessening of anguish; a deadening of humanity. One has heard now a thousand times the words of condemnation, certainly sincere and heartfelt, employed by politicians, clergymen, and other public figures when something particularly revolting has happened. They have become almost meaningless: the vocabulary has been exhausted. 'Terrorist', 'murderer', 'diabolical', 'dastardly outrage', 'cowardly crime': what other words can the poor men use? But the currency has been devalued; not just the currency of the words; the currency of the concepts, too. I am sure this is so of the individuals who commit the murders, who plant the bombs; otherwise no degree of idealism, whether in the cause of 'a Free Ireland' or in the cause of 'our Protestant heritage', could allow them to persevere without falling victims themselves to nausea, hysteria, and collapse. There is a protective mechanism for them too. Unhappily, if the rest of us are to survive without losing our reason, we must allow our own emotional reactions to be devalued. It is possible that all those who survive the Ulster Troubles of the 1970s will be morally or emotionally crippled for the rest of their lives. But I hope, and choose to believe, otherwise; just as a whole generation could return from the slaughter of each of the world wars without (as it seems to me) any perceptible loss of humanity, so (it seems to me) when this plague has passed by — and sooner or later, somehow, it must — the survivors will return to a more human level of sensibility.

FOUR

In the year of William Brett's death, my great-great-great-great-great-grandfather, Bernard Brett, was twenty-two, and had already made an early marriage: his wife was Katherine Montgomery, a younger daughter of a County Down family of considerable standing. A kinsman of hers wrote, about 1696, of her and her elder sister, 'Then is Katherin marryed to Mr Barnard Brett of Ballynewport in Lecahill; both the said named sisters are good wives and have kind husbands (which is a sign of wive's complacency), their father consenting to their wedlocks, and give-ing his blessing to them'. The young couple set up home at Erenagh, a substantial house, less than a mile from Ballynewport, which had been built thirty years earlier by a relation of Katherine's mother. Bernard farmed in a small way, and also held a paid commission in the standing militia. In 1708 he was lieutenant in Colonel Nicholas Price's troop of horse; by 1715 he was captain commanding one of the fifteen companies of foot into which the County Militia was divided. Until calamity fell upon him in his fifty-second year, he seems to have lived a quiet and comfortable life as a modest country gentleman. During this time he and Katherine had three children, William, born in 1692; Mary, in 1695; and Charles, in 1698.

His elder brother Jasper, who inherited all the family lands, had taken holy orders in 1692; in the following year he was appointed curate of Ballyculter by his cousin Ward (the Special Visitation of that year reports alarmingly *deest calix* – 'the chalice has gone missing'); and in the same year married Mary McNeill, daughter of the Dean of Down and grand-daughter of Archbishop Marsh. With such connections, Jasper prospered in the Church: from 1699 till 1707 he was Rector of Killyleagh: from 1707 till 1713, Prebendary, presumably absentee, of Rasharkin in County Antrim: from 1709 till his death, Vicar of Rathmullan, the parish in which Ballynewport was situated (he also held the curacies of the nearby parishes of Bright and Tyrella): and from 1713 till his death, Chancellor of the cathedral of Connor. He was, in short, a pluralist and a squarson; but he seems to have taken some at least of his duties seriously: he was very hot against 'clandestine marriages': he published a cogent, if ineffectual, pamphlet against smuggling entitled *The Sin of With-holding Tribute, by Running of Goods, Concealing Exise, Etc.*; and he seems to have been of a missionary turn of mind. According to the later account of a distant cousin, 'Jasper Brett caused all his tenants to attend Rathmullan church; and there are now a good many Murphys, Magraws, etc. who are *Hot* orangemen, whose forefathers were Roman Catholics'.

Unhappily, however, Jasper's successful career in the Church was not matched by equal success in handling his financial affairs, or for that matter his family. True, the eldest son, John, turned out well; he followed his father into the Church, took a radical and ecumenical view of Church politics – in 1735 he wrote: '"Tis however one great blessing that attends the present Age that the Sourness and Rancour amongst divided Christians, which hath been so long the Bane of Society and the Great Scandal of Christianity, is gradually decaying and dying away' – (how was he to foresee the several varieties of 'Sourness and Rancour' displayed by Dr Ian Paisley, the Rev. Martin Smyth, the Rev. William Beattie, and Father Denis Faul, a quarter-millennium later?); was the author of numerous sermons and pamphlets on subjects sacred, political, and profane; and held a number of comfortable livings in various parts of Ireland. But the second son, Matthew, was a black sheep, whose misdeeds as an attorney's apprentice in Dublin caused his father endless worry; the youngest, Cromwell (named after the Ardglass neighbours, not after Oliver Protector), could only find employment as a 'guager' in the Excise in the farthest wilds of Galway; and his daughter, Mary, married an impecunious captain of Dragoons. These family worries, however, were vastly increased by money troubles. How far these were due to Jasper's own extravagance, it is hard to tell; he is said to have kept open house on a grand scale at Ballynewport, constantly entertaining the neighbouring gentry and the officers stationed in the district. A number of turnip-shaped wine bottles, with 'I Brett' impressed in the glass, were excavated from the former cellars of Ballynewport house about 1845: the last of these was given to, and treasured by, my great-grandfather, and finally destroyed by the bomb of May 1972.

Jasper inherited the family estate heavily encumbered by his father's debts. In 1703 the executors were forced to sell off three townlands from William Brett's estate 'to preserve the rest in his name and blood by reason that the whole estate will not pay the interest of the money due thereon'; the sale brought in almost £2,000 but Jasper received only £213 of this, the rest going to extinguish part – but only part – of his father's debts. For twenty years he struggled on under an ever-increasing load of debts and mortgages; but by 1723 he could stave off disaster no longer. It was agreed that he and his family should leave Ballynewport and remove to a house leased from the Wards, in the nearby village of Killough: his younger brother Bernard was to take over the estate and, with the help of new loans from his rich Montgomery father-in-law and others, pay off some of Jasper's debts, and try to set matters on their feet again. These arrangements were negotiated by Michael Ward, an efficient Dublin barrister, later to become Judge Ward, and by young Charles Brett, not long qualified as a solicitor. Much correspondence survives from this period, and the next few years; the letters demonstrate the complexity, but do not do much to illuminate the causes, of Bernard Brett's tangled affairs. His health began to deteriorate: in 1723 a Killough worthy reported to Michael Ward: 'I came here on Thursday sennight to Mr Brett in a most violent quotidian ague. The cold and hot fitts held for 12 in every 24 hours & he raved very much. He has had no fitts but a grievous bloody flux since Thursday last'. And his letters become gradually more and more gloomy. From them, one gets the feeling of a small close-knit community in County Down, everyone related by marriage to almost everyone else, almost everyone in debt to everyone else.

Bernard owed money, amongst others, to a Mr Partinton, who was becoming importunate, and to Mr Jolly, a minor employee of the Wards who was also lieutenant in Brett's company of militia. His attempts to improve the yield and value of his land by spreading marl on it were unsuccessful, for he lacked the necessary capital to complete the job. In May 1725 he wrote to Michael Ward explaining his position at some length, and with considerable candour:

> The great uneasyness I lye under, and the many insults I meet with by being in Debt and haveing other people obliged for parts of it, is little removed from abject Slavery. For tho' I be determined upon the sale of Ballynewport (after which I can demonstrate my self to be worth a thousand pounds besides my Imployment, clear of all debt) yet that can not be done so speedily, without great loss in the sale, and some discredit which can only be prevented by making the sale of it an act of choice and not of compulsion. . . . I am at present press'd for money.

At this point he received timely assistance from both his father-in-law and his cousin; new mortgages over the Ballynewport lands in favour of both were registered soon after. Things were tided over for a few years more.

In fact, in 1727, it looked very much as though his affairs had taken a turn for the better. He was given charge of the rebuilding of the cavalry barracks at Killough, and hoped for a profit from it. And, a real stroke of luck, he succeeded in arranging a most satisfactory marriage for his eldest son, William: best of all, he was to receive himself a cash payment of £600 for the young lady's dowry. The match was entirely suitable. Jane Major was the daughter of a Protestant widow from Drogheda. William was a clergyman though evidently foppish and indolent: he did not receive promotion beyond the rank of curate till he was over sixty: he ended up as a vicar choral of both St Patrick's and Christ Church cathedrals, Dublin; perhaps this is evidence of a redeeming musical talent.

This somewhat ne'er-do-well clergyman died in Dublin in May 1764: was it perhaps from him that there has come down in the family a treasured heirloom? Jonathan Swift, Dean of St Patrick's, died on Saturday 19 October 1745. 'He was laid out in his own hall, and great crowds went to see him. His coffin was open; he had on his head neither cap nor wig; there was not much hair on the front or very top, but it was long and thick behind, very white, and was like flax on the pillow. Mrs Barnard, his nursetender, sat at his head; but having occasion to leave the room for a short time some person cut a lock of hair from his head, which she missed upon her return, and after that day no person was admitted to see him'. I have on my table as I write a square of black-edged paper, inscribed 'Dean Swift's Hair' in faded ink, in which is enclosed a lock of hair, 'very white', 'like flax', neatly tied in a knot of thin red string.

The Articles of Agreement on young William's marriage concluded with a declaration that 'it will be convenient for some time, that we should all live together, not only for the mutual support & comfort of each other, but also, that we may use our joynt endeavours to lessen any incumbrances that may be upon the said estate'. So the happy pair moved in with their hard-up parents at Ballynewport. There is no record, I am sorry to say, of how they all got on together. The dowry money proved insufficient to stem the decline in Bernard Brett's finances. In May 1728 he was in difficulties again, and soliciting Judge Ward's support for an application to Lord Limerick for help. 'If you will seriously reflect upon the hard fate of my father's family, that way I hope I shall have your helping hand'. Was this an oblique reference to the money old William Brett had lost at cards to his Ward cousins? Things went gradually from bad to worse: the times were very bad; 'in 1727–30, one bad season followed another, there was absolute disaster – the old and sick "dying and rotting by cold and famine and filth and vermin"; the younger labourers so enfeebled by lack of food that even when they could find employment they had no strength to work'. Although things were somewhat better in the northern counties of Ireland than in the south and west, they were bad enough, and it is hardly surprising that Bernard Brett, overloaded with his own debts on top of those incurred by his father and his elder brother, could not make the remaining acres at Ballynewport pay.

The end came in October 1731, when Bernard Brett slipped away from home and took ship to the Isle of Man to evade his creditors. The contents of his house were seized by Judge Ward's agent, and an inventory (still in existence) prepared. The valuation came to a total of £33 23s. 11d.; but as to 'the several blanks in the inventory, the goods are to be valued by weight, or belonging to Captain Johnston. Mrs. Brett would not let the valuers, which was old Mrs Feattus and her husband, value them less – I am afraid they will not sell for so much, I told her so, she said she was not afraid to sell them at it'. One can only admire the fortitude with which Katherine Brett fought a rear-guard action on her husband's behalf.

The Isle of Man was still, at this period, a place of refuge for those pursued by creditors, as well as a haven for smugglers. It remained outside the jurisdiction both of the British and Irish courts and customs authorities. Indeed, it 'served as a veritable metropolis of illegal trade': wine, spirits, tea, and tobacco were smuggled into Ireland, wool was smuggled out in very large quantities to avoid the restrictions on the Irish woollen trade imposed by Westminster in 1699. The coast of Lecale was a mere thirty miles from the Isle of Man, and Bernard Brett almost certainly made the passage in one of the smuggling smacks that used the beach at Tyrella, only two or three miles from Ballynewport.

He was to spend the rest of his life – nine years – on the Isle of Man. I do not know whether he ever saw any of his family again after his disgrace. Katherine stayed behind in Killough in a house rented from Judge Ward; probably she received help from her own family, the Montgomeries; in 1745 Judge Ward's agent wrote despairingly, 'Old Mrs Brett, whenever I ask her for rent, She desires me to distrain her poor tenants; Mr Hall's rent and one more that pays well she receives herself. I desired she would allow Mr Hall to pay me, and take the rest to herself, but she would not consent. I am at a loss how to behave with her, for she doth not care to part with a penny'. This has the determined ring of the lady who refused to allow the valuers to place any but her own price on her husband's furniture

Bernard Brett eked out an existence in Castletown by means of remittances from Judge Ward and the Judge's brother-in-law Lord Ikerrin, and from Lord Limerick, grandson of the builder of Erinagh and a cousin of Katherine Brett. It is clear that Judge Ward treated him not unkindly; in April 1732, only six months after the flit, his agent reported that he had duly remitted £50 'to Mr Bernard Brett as you ordered'. A pathetic letter, written to Judge Ward in April 1738 from Castletown, conveys little enthusiasm for the suggestion that he might, at the age of sixty-seven, return to Ireland and take a job under the Revenue Commissioners. It is the last letter of his to survive:

My Good Ld,
It is now more than time for me to acknowledge yr constant and repeated favours to me, without which, I must freely owne, I cou'd not subsist; for tho I must owne with great gratitude that I have recd particular favours from many friends, yet my main support has ever been from you, which I am never to be sufficiently thankfull for, nor can I make any other return but my darly and fervent prayers to God for the well-being of you and your dear family. I had a hint given to me that yr Lordsp was of opinion I ought to go over; my inclinations are good if I knew where to go. I had a letter with a present from my good Ld Limerick last July, wherein he told me that he had recommended me to one of the Commissioners, but desired me not to mention it to anyone till he cou'd find what effect it would have, but I never heard more of it since.
But when I consider I am now 67 years old, it would not be easy to get an Imployment in the Revenue, that I cou'd be capable of executing; nor cou'd I refuse anything that were offered me without rejecting the endeavours of that Noble Ld to serve me, which is a shocking consideration. And considering the great troubles I have undergone, I cannot be supposed to live long; and to involve myselfe anew in the affairs of the world Just at the close of my days, when in all probability I shall not have long to prepare for an endless duration, is a thing that often perplexes my thoughts. Indeed, if I cou'd hope for any thing by which I cou'd hope to make my poor children the better, I shou'd think it my indispencible duty, both to God and to them, to spend my

old carcass to the last thread, and to ease my friends of the burthen of my support.

Tis true I have lived here seven years by a providence that is next to a miracle, and tho very often without clothes to cover my nakedness and but a goats Hare Wigg to cover my head, I can without vanity and with some comfort say, that I have the universal esteem of everyone; and more especially our worthy Governor, who has distinguished me from all strangers in this Isle, and has oblyged me to dyne with him every Sunday since ever he came over. He is a man of great humanity, sobriety and worth, and tis a great trouble to me that I have no friend of distinction that knows him, that cou'd take notice of his civility to me. I have now tired yr lordsp, and will only add that I am to yr Lordsp and family

> My Dr Ld
> a most obedient and most
> affectt humble Sert
>
> Ber. Brett

The 'goats Hare Wigg' is a particularly touching image of an eighteenth-century gentleman in pecuniary distress (goats' hair being the cheapest and nastiest material, used only for the most inferior kind of wig); shabby clothes must be endured, but to have gone bare-headed would have been to abandon the very last symbol of gentility. And, after all, Bernard Brett's father had been a gentleman of standing and High Sheriff of his county.

I have been able to discover no record of the life that he lived in the Isle of Man: only of his death there. The parish register of Malew, in which Castletown was then situated, contains an entry showing the burial on 14 August 1740 of 'Captain Barnet Brett'. Though he must have died in lonely and impoverished obscurity, though his Christian name is wrongly given, it is at least a solace to know that he managed to retain his military rank, like his wig, to the end.

FIVE

My own childhood was not in Lecale, but in the northern part of County Down; always within sight of Belfast Lough and the constant processions of shipping coming and going; one had only to climb Craigantlet hill to enjoy a wide view out over the North Channel – Kintyre, Ailsa Craig, Galloway; on clear days, even the Isle of Man, the place of exile of poor Bernard Brett. I liked ships and the sea then, I like them still. Holidays were for the most part spent at Portballintrae, on the Atlantic-facing coast of County Antrim, a then almost-unspoiled fishing village strung around its horseshoe-shaped sandy bay. Along the beaches and below the cliffs of that marvellous coastline I learned the arts of damming the cold rock-streams, and of building castles and fortified towns worthy of Viollet-le-Duc. These arts I practise still; the secret is, of course, to use a full-size garden spade, never the foolish and flimsy spades of tin or plastic, which are the best that seaside toyshops can provide.

When I was nine, I was sent off to boarding school in Yorkshire, not far from my kind maternal grandparents. I was, on the whole, very happy there. I read enormously, and learned from a brilliant and sympathetic teacher – Patric Dickinson. the poet – to enjoy books, and especially poetry; I learned also to detest organised games of every kind. This foible was looked on with surprising tolerance, and I was often allowed to find other occupations for myself. The school was on the edge of the dales, and I have recollections of long hot summer days spent with sketch-book and water-colour box on the hillsides; also of the winter of the great snow, when we built a village of igloos; mine was the village pub; bar, inn-sign, and all. I was not the only Irish boy in the school, and – apart from sprouting shamrock on St Patrick's day – was conscious of no difference from the English, and many Scottish, boys. This changed somewhat after the outbreak of war. There was a definite social distinction attaching to the sea-voyage, undertaken alone, particularly after the loss of the cross-channel packet *Munster* with all hands and all passengers, mined at the mouth of the Mersey in 1940.

In due course I went to Rugby. I was not happy there. Between 1941 and 1945 all the younger masters were away at the war; some of the teachers were hoary shellbacks brought back from retirement. The rationed food was atrocious; heating and hot water were alike in short supply; life was Spartan, and the prevailing code of heartiness did not at all suit my tastes. I was seen by some at least of my contemporaries as a frivolous and despicable Irishman (neutrality in the war being not approved of) lacking seriousness and a proper appreciation of the team spirit. My housemaster was an elderly bachelor clergyman: he and I did not see eye to eye. My father was sympathetic, and took my part in the more significant of my conflicts with authority: he had hated school himself. Indeed, he says that in the trenches during the First World War he used to wake with relief from nightmares that he was back at school. He had chosen to send me to Rugby, he told me, for two reasons: the teaching was good — which it was — and he hoped that it would instil into me a social conscience and a sense of responsibility to the community. It did indeed: and when, later on, I joined the Labour Party, he may have felt that he had got a little more than he had bargained for.

*   *   *   *

Just as Bernard Brett had served in the militia, so, during the second half of the war, my father served in the Home Guard. He had attained the rank of Captain, and an M.C., in France with the Connaught Rangers during the 1914–18 war: but in the Home Guard he held the rank of Sergeant. In Northern Ireland it had much in common with, but a flavour distinctively different from, the popular image of Dad's Army. To begin with, there were not enough khaki uniforms to go round; so the volunteers of Ulster — being farthest from the invaders — were issued with uniforms that, for some unfathomable reason, had been dyed black. The new corps was accordingly known throughout the countryside as 'the Blackguards'. The first set of black battle-dress issued to my father was twice too large for him; he and I demonstrated that we could both fit into that infinitely capacious pair of black trousers at the same time. The Home Guard was unlike Bernard Brett's militia in that Catholics were welcomed, and indeed joined it in some numbers. I think my father greatly enjoyed the opportunity to break across pre-war social barriers and get to know on an equal footing neighbours from very different backgrounds.

Before long, he was appointed intelligence officer for North Down, and issued with a ration of petrol for his well-loved Riley car. When I was home from school, I often accompanied him on his visits to the units scattered over the countryside. It was in this way that I came to know a young farmer from the Ards named Andrew Bailie, with whom I used to spend many weeks of my holidays.

*   *   *   *

Andrew was the youngest son of a large family. His father had died not long before I met him first; his elder brothers and sisters had all moved away (though to no great distance) in search of jobs or husbands; he was then unmarried, and he was seeking to work the farm at Black-abbey in accordance with the most up-to-date principles of the Young Farmers' Clubs, of which he was an enthusiastic member. My father shrewdly saw that I had too little occupation during school holidays, and sent me to make myself useful to Andrew for weeks or months at a time. This was a new world to me: an old-fashioned County Down farmhouse, using oil-lamps for want of electricity, and a privy without running water. Life was lived in the farm kitchen; at dinner-time the two labourers joined the family for great meals of fry, or stew, potatoes, home-baked bread and butter, and tea, sitting on old motor-car seats round the scrubbed table in front of the blackened range. 'The room' — stuffy and dusty, an uncomfortable kind of formal parlour — was no more used than the front door; both served only for funerals or the visits of the Presbyterian minister; the kitchen door opened directly onto the farmyard, and all life was lived on that axis. I learned to work the levers of an old-fashioned binder; to drive a tractor; to make hay, and silage; to attend to the health of calves and pigs; to milk a cow; to bottle milk.

After a week or two spent at Blackabbey, my clothes and I smelled richly of manure, silage, and the soil. This my mother did not much care for; so my father arranged that on my way home I should call first at his office, where I could have a bath and change into clean clothes. The office bath-room was a kind of urban counterpart to the world of rural oil-lamps I had just left. Though on the mezzanine floor, it really formed part of the caretaker's quarters: I doubt if there has ever been another partner in the firm who has taken a bath there. The bath-tub itself, stained with rust, framed in faded mahogany, had corrugations running at right-angles to its length; these left most peculiar ridges-and-furrows on the backside. Outside the bathroom door were three articles of furniture that much intrigued me. The first was a very large aspidistra in a pot: I am glad to say that it has survived three years spent out of doors after our bomb, and is still flourishing; it must now be well over 100 years old. The second was a rickety glass case on spindly legs, known as 'Exhibit A', containing positively nothing except layer upon layer of ancient dust: one could count back to see which years had been vintage years: it was explained to me that this had originally been great-grandfather's fern-case, but the ferns (less hardy than the aspidistra) had long since expired. Third, and best, was a beautifully made ship-builder's model of an Edwardian steam-yacht, the *Lady Blanche*; every detail was perfect, down to the boat-hooks lying on the thwarts of the lifeboats swinging by block and tackle from their davits. The model was damaged by flying glass in 1972, but my father laboriously repaired and re-rigged it: and it stands once again in the office for the enjoyment of juvenile clients and visitors. These furnishings are linked for ever in my mind with the home-coming from the farm, the transition from country to town.

Blackabbey had more to teach me than just the mechanical skills of agriculture. The farm-house was always boiling with brothers, sisters, cousins, nephews, nieces, and neighbours. The family adhered to the Scots traditions of East Ulster; I attended Presbyterian services in Greyabbey church; I also attended Young Farmers' bun-fights, and badminton evenings organised by the Church of Ireland rector in Ballywalter village hall. Rather daringly, Monopoly was played (not for money) by lamp-light on the kitchen table on winter evenings. But alcohol was never countenanced —was indeed feared; I came to recognise the gulf that separated the respectable farmer, owning his own land and terrified of losing it, from the feckless and through-other labourer who drank the week's wages in the village pub, and then went home to terrorise his wife and children. I learned to understand, though not to speak, the Lallans dialect (closely similar to that of Galloway) of that countryside. I learned too to respect, though not to share, the political and religious opinions and prejudices, strictly conventional and unalterable, of this community of Irish descendants of Scots settlers. Above all, I learned to love the land and soil of County Down.

Blackabbey was a farm of 100 acres or so, in the hills on the spine of the Ards peninsula, here some five miles wide. The cold outer sea of the

North Channel washed the sands and reefs of Ballywalter; the warmer inner sea of Strangford Lough washed the muddier shore of Greyabbey; the farm lay half-way between the two. It was a site redolent of history, yet the history was kept always at arm's length. In Greyabbey stand the imposing remains of the Cistercian abbey founded by John de Courcy in 1193. But at Blackabbey nothing remains of the Benedictine abbey founded by de Courcy three years earlier. Andrew told me once, as we were harrowing the long field in the valley south of the farmhouse, that in his father's day the plough had turned up here a series of carved and inscribed slabs of stone, and a cavity as of the foundations of a room. But they had speedily destroyed and buried all they found, for fear that they might lose the use of good land to prying and ridiculous archaeologists from Belfast. It was a lesson that I took to heart.

After his father's death, Andrew set about improving and modernising both farm and farmhouse. New sheds were built; concrete was laid; electricity, a bathroom, and a flushing lavatory were installed; fields were drained; a pedigree Ayrshire bull was bought, with attendant purebred cows and heifers. Andrew married, his own children were born. For a few years the farm prospered, and I came to have a proper appreciation of the finer points of Ayrshire cattle — surely the handsomest and most beautifully coloured beasts of any breed. But alas, Andrew over-reached himself financially; those who bought his milk, and those who bought his calves, were more interested in quantity than quality; and in the end the farm had to be sold. Andrew died, still very young, a few years later: his funeral was a moving occasion I shall always remember, for with Andrew was buried a great part of my boyhood. The young Minister, with flowing hair, gave a lengthy address by the graveside; he belonged to that verbose and oratorical tradition of Presbyterianism I find distasteful; I prefer the austere and seemly understatement of the once-established Church. But on that windy hillside stood all the neighbouring farmers whom I had known in my youth, and the farm labourers too; I shall always remember Big Sandy weeping like a child while he recalled to me what a good master Andrew had been.

*   *   *   *

The Ards peninsula is very beautiful, especially the west-facing shore that looks out across the grey waters of Strangford Lough to the distant

Mourne mountains. It is not really my own territory, I suppose, for my forebears came from Lecale, on the other side of the fast and narrow tide-rip that drains and refills the Lough. But it is a country very close to my heart. And perhaps there are family links too.

Very late at night on 8 January 1574 a certain Lieutenant Jerome Brett sat in Ardkeen Castle (a few miles from Blackabbey) writing a report to his superior officer in Dublin, Lord Fitzwilliam. Ten days earlier he had been ordered by Sir Thomas Smith, Queen Elizabeth's private secretary, to occupy the castle: but the whole expedition was going amiss: the Savages and O'Neills to whom this territory belonged had put up a stronger resistance than expected: Sir Thomas's son, leader of the expedition, had been murdered here by his own trusted retainers three months earlier. Jerome Brett wrote that a strong party of horsemen and kern had taken up position around Ardkeen, probably with a view to an ambush; that they had fortunately been sighted by his men, who had fired a cannon from their boat; that Raymond Savage had then come up, offering many courtesies, which were however 'lacrime crokedilis'; and that Brett had managed to arrest and bring into the castle one Partick Hazard, 'a notorious treytor & a murderer', as to whose fate he sought instructions. But the night was not over; in the early hours, Jerome Brett was obliged to add a postscript: 'Even as & whylst I was writing my letter at midnight suddenly slipped Patrick Hazard his foot out of irons, & leapt out of the Castle of Ardkeen such a leap as, if he had been condemned, I had for his death as lief have given him that leap as the gallows; yet he dyd it'. His prisoner had got clean away.

There is no castle today at Ardkeen; only the foundations and a few stone stairs of the tower-house survive. But the site is an evocative one. Just as the Ards is a peninsula almost detached from the rest of Ireland, so Ardkeen is a peninsula almost cut off from the Ards: a drumlin gone paddling out into the tidal waters of Strangford Lough. Today it is isolated and deserted. The farm track along the shore leads to a hill surmounted by grassy earthworks: the remains of a Norman motte, possibly incorporating a much earlier rath: a bailey on the landward side, bounded by a semi-circular ditch and rampart: a grassy saucer at the summit of the mound: on its seaward lip, the foundations of the castle. To the southward, under the shelter of the hill, stand the roofless walls of Ardkeen church, built in the thirteenth century but roofless since the Great Wind of 1839. In the graveyard are many memorials of the eighteenth century, a few of the seventeeth century, and a single much-worn stone coffin-lid carved with a Norman sword.

It is in places such as this that history takes on a directly personal character for me. I am conscious that no great number of lives divides me in time, no distance at all divides me in place, from human beings with whom I have much in common, to whom perhaps I owe much. I do not find it impossible to share in imagination the feelings of Jerome Brett, besieged and his prisoner newly escaped, in his stone room on the summit of Ardkeen in the small hours of a winter's night just over 400 years ago.

SIX

Charles Brett, my great-great-great-great-grandfather, qualified as a solicitor about 1720. I do not know where he served his apprenticeship; probably in Dublin, like his slightly younger cousin Matt Brett, who was articled to 'Mr Anderson, Clerk in the Chief Remembrancer's Office'. He does not seem at first to have set up in practice, but to have lived at home with his parents, first at Erinagh, then at Ballynewport. He played an active part in the elaborate financial negotiations in which Bernard, Jasper, and Judge Ward were involved in 1723–4.

Charles was aged thirty-three when the family's affairs crashed in 1731 and his father had to flee to the Isle of Man from his creditors. His position was an unenviable one. His elder brother William was plainly useless; his uncle Jasper had largely contributed to the downfall by his extravagance; his mother was left without means; the family's creditors had moved in and sold up everything they could lay hands on. Perhaps he received some support and assistance from his mother's family, the Montgomeries, but they had lost money by his father's bankruptcy, as had the only other possible patron to whom he could turn, Judge Ward. He seems to have set to with courage to mend his affairs as best he could. When the opportunity came his way – perhaps not very often – he practised his profession. He took such small part-time employments as were open to him: he was appointed Registrar to the Down Royal Corporation of Horse Breeders, which organised the horse races at Downpatrick, at a salary of £5 a year (paid sometimes two or three years in arrears). He also acted, at one time or another, as clerk to the local Turnpike Trustees; registrar of the diocese of Down; a notary public for the county; and, in his latter years, seneschal of the manor court of Bangor. Many years later, in 1822, his son was to write of him:

He was a man of such sweetness of temper and who had the happy art of making himself so universally beloved; that his society and acquaintance were eagerly sought after by all persons of rank and consequence in the two counties of Down and Antrim amongst whom he lived much, and by whom he was appointed to several employments by which he was enabled to support the character of an independent Gentleman.

This account, though no doubt rather partial, seems to be borne out by the quite copious correspondence that survives from his later years. His letters show him as an able man; shrewd, intelligent, and industrious. In addition to the various minor public employments he secured, he acted as factor or land agent for several local families. His home was at Killough, and he farmed there in a very small way on land leased from Judge Ward; but his various employments took him much away from home – to Dublin, Belfast, Drogheda, Lisburn, Bangor, and Downpatrick. In 1739 the agent who looked after the Ward family estate at Bangor died, and Judge Ward appointed Charles Brett to the post; four years later the agent at Killough died also, and the judge decided to combine the two posts. From this time on, Charles Brett's regular letters and reports to the Judge throw much light on the state of the country, and show their author in an attractive light as a humane and sympathetic agent, not at all afraid to stand up to his employer on behalf of a deserving tenant.

These were very hard times in the countryside. In Ireland, as in most of Western Europe, 1740 and 1741 were years of absolute disaster; Michael Drake has written, 'It is possible that the mortality of those years was never repeated even during the Great Famine of 1845–7. The horror of the 1840s seemed so much greater because it occurred in a Europe that had all but banished subsistence crises'. The famine started with a hard frost, which set in just after Christmas 1739, continued for seven weeks without a break, and almost totally destroyed the potato crop. The summer that followed was cold and wet; the ensuing winter was a bitter one also; crops failed, cattle and horses died for lack of fodder, and starvation was followed by outbreaks of typhus and dysentery. A Dublin pamphleteer wrote in 1741:

It is computed by some, and perhaps not without reason, that as many people have died of want, and disorder occasioned by want, within these two years past, as fell by the sword in the massacre and rebellion of '41. Whole parishes have in some places been almost desolated; and the dead have been eaten in the fields by dogs for want of people to bury them. Whole thousands have perished, some of hunger, and other of disorders occasioned by unnatural, unwholesome and putrid diet.

The country recovered only slowly; in 1744 Charles Brett wrote to Judge Ward: 'Cattle dying by thousands in the County of Antrim, I'm afraid it will soon be here, for we have no food'. And in the following year: 'We are in a melancholy condition here, famine is beginning to stare at us. Wheat is nine shillings the hundred & I much doubt whether there is as much sound oats in the parish as will sow it, a great part of the harvest not being gather'd till late October'. And economic worries were not the only ones: politically the country remained unsettled, and the activities of the Jacobite party and the King over the water kept the Protestant gentry in constant dread of another rising or civil war. In April 1743 a small warship, the *Litchfield,* was wrecked at Kilclief, a few miles from Castleward, and Robert Ward wrote anxiously to his brother:

> There was 40 barrels of gunpowder in ye ship cast away at Kilclief all of which is carryed off by ye country folk (but damaged); they have also got a good number of Muskets etc. out of the three last ships that were cast away, & it is more than probable that the Papists have got the best share of both. I shall doe all in my power to discover them . . . round Lecale are most if not all Papists, I am told they have good share of fire arms.

Charles Brett's letters naturally deal more with day-to-day questions of estate management than with affairs of national importance. There is much discussion of timber, trespassers, the letting of mosses (peat bogs), and the making and renewal of leases. In 1744 he was urging Judge Ward to grant a new lease to an old tenant, James Blackwood:

> It was never known that you treated an old tenant with disregard who did not manifestly deserve it, and I venture to assure you that his good wishes for you and your family are very sincere, and that he will always deserve your countenance. I have wrote upon this affair rather like a Solicitor than a servant, for wh. I must, and do, implore your indulgence.

In 1746, from Killough:

> The tenants are miserably reduced by the calamities of the last two years, & none of them except Lyons (the tenant at Castlehill) have any the least knowledge or genius to husbandry; and even he must have been undone had I not lent him £25 in April '45 to enable him to

stock and labour the ground; the winter before having swept away his whole stock, and I yet unpaid.

And in 1749, of an unfortunate tenant named James Dennison:

The arrear is £61. 4s. 0d. and if calamities of an uncommon nature had not visited the poor man for two years successively, so large an arrear out of so small a rent would never have happened. He was twice left without a living beast, & summer was twelve months he and his whole family above six weeks in a Rageing Fever; and as I have now some reason to believe he will remit, I hope you will accept of this method of being paid, rather than set him adrift.

Finally, the letters contain items of personal news, and sometimes sheer gossip: from Bangor, in 1752: 'The old postwoman, which was a very good one, is disabled by age & poverty & there is no-one in her place who are not idle and drunken — one McCrea her son-in-law took up her place & Mr Leach, poor man, hath taken it into his head to debauch the man with whisky, and his wife with his embraces'. And, of a Scotsman proposing himself as a tenant: 'a very idle spark, and hath marry'd a Scotch Gentlewoman too proud to work: she a drinker of tea, and he of drams and ale'.

At last, in 1749, aged over fifty, Charles Brett felt that he had re-established himself sufficiently securely to contemplate marriage. A single rather touching letter to his intended wife survives: it is dated from Drogheda, past one in the morning, 21 January 1749:

My dear Molly Carr,
    The excessive badness of the weather kept me here last night, and tho' it prevented me proceeding so far on my journey as to be in Dublin early tomorrow, yet, my life, I am in hopes of being with you on Saturday next. But lest any cross accident should prevent me, I would have you in the mean time employ yourself in settling your mother's and your affairs, and making such a plan of them as will enable you and I when we meet to put them in such a method as will best secure you and at the same time give her a satisfactory subsistence; in order to which I beg you will be as favourable to her side of the question as your filial piety in its fullest latitude can possibly prompt you.

These, my dearest Molly, are my sentiments on this matter, and as you are the best judge of her and your circumstances, it is upon that judgement, as in every other affair of my life, I mean to be determined. You and she have a right to this upon mere mercantile principles, and I should think you thrown away upon a man who would but barely act up to that. . . .
May God protect you, I am ever yours.

The trip to Dublin evidently took much longer than anticipated; a couple of months later Charles Brett wrote to Judge Ward from Bangor: 'My journey to Dublin has in the last degree distressed me in my farming, both here and at Killough, my servants and horses being yet there, and I here rather idle and grieved for want of them. I can't possibly help myself till they come to me'. The marriage must nevertheless have taken place soon after. Molly Carr was the daughter of a merchant in Downpatrick. She was not perhaps in her first youth. Many years later, her only son Charles was to write of her: 'To say of her that she was the best of daughters: wives: and mothers, would only give a partial view of this incomparable woman. She was possessed of a masculine understanding (which made the Rev. Humphrey Adams say "Molly Carr has brains") joined to the utmost suavity of manners: joined to a lively and cheerful flow of wit and humour: unmixed with anything sarcastic or satireacal: happy in her domestic attentions, to her aged mother, her husband whom she adored, and her child'. It seems to have been a very happy, though not a long-lived, marriage. A daughter, Charity, was born in 1751, but died in infancy; their son Charles was born in 1752, at Bangor Castle. In April 1758 Charles Brett was at Killough, and evidently ill, for he added a codicil to an earlier will, appointing Rev. Bernard Ward an additional Executor and Guardian. He died, aged sixty, three weeks later, and was buried at Killough.

SEVEN

I do not suppose that my own war-time schooldays differed much from those of many of my contemporaries from similar middle-class backgrounds. Belfast was heavily blitzed in 1941, and I was at home during the biggest of the raids; but the bombs were falling some eight miles away in the city, so I remember principally the fireworks aspect of the event. (This seems to be the raid described by Anthony Powell in *The Soldier's Art*.) Because of the land border with neutral Eire, the flavour of war was rather different from that in mainland Britain. A good deal of food found its way north over that border; many people went on shopping expeditions to Dublin and returned with lavish additions to their rations. This was viewed with deep disapproval by conventional persons. In the first place, it was disloyal. In the second place, it was unfair. In the third place, there was the risk that one might be entrapped by the German spies and U-boat Captains who were believed to haunt every bar and restaurant in 'the Free State'. Nevertheless, a good deal of barter went on; an elderly client from County Kildare used to come north once a year in order to exchange great chunks of raw steak for his favourite reading-matter – last year's telephone directory.

Travel permits were required by all those over the age of sixteen seeking to cross between England and Ireland. Long, weary midnight queues of travellers stood in the blacked-out stations of Heysham, Liverpool, and Stranraer, waiting to have their credentials scrutinised. These were examined slowly and with scepticism: if tall for one's age, one had to produce a birth certificate to prove that one was under sixteen. Like many other Anglo-Ulstermen of that generation, to this day I carry my birth certificate – cracked, brown, and torn – in the back of my wallet. It is a comfort if one suffers a passing *crise d'identité*; though of course, it requires an act of faith to be sure that one is still the same person as the infant whose birth is so succinctly recorded.

Because of its distance from the Continent, Ulster harboured some colonies of a kind not so common elsewhere. The first wave of these comprised the civilian population of Gibraltar. The next was a multilingual wave of seamen – Free French, Free Dutch, Free Belgian, Free Norwegian, Free Poles, and so on – from the warships escorting the convoys of the western approaches. (I was startled a few years later, when I first got a job in Paris, to be greeted by my new boss with the words: '*Ah, vous venez de Belfast. Vous êtes, sans doute, comme moi membre du Tramvays Club de Belfast?*' The Tramwaymen's Club was a drinking den near the docks, which welcomed the navies of the world with unstinted hospitality.) The third was a wave of raw young soldiers from the American Middle West: Ireland was their first landfall in Europe, and here they were acclimatised for a few months before going on to more arduous theatres of war. I remember most the sense of social strain when two gum-chewing members of this visiting army, on their best behaviour, came to share high tea with us. And finally, there were the melancholy German prisoners of war who, after the departure of the Americans, came to occupy the Nissen huts in the wooden glen between our house and the sea. These I found less sympathetic than the Italian prisoners in whose company, as a patriotic duty, I picked potatoes in the Warwickshire fields during half-holidays from school.

There loomed over me the prospect of military service. I thought I should have liked the navy, but my eyesight was not good enough; except for the paymaster's branch; that did not sound much fun. There was, indeed, no conscription in Northern Ireland. This was a sensible decision; very many thousands of volunteers joined the British forces from Ireland, north and south; but to have applied compulsory service to the republicans of the north would have courted civil war at home, and treachery in the field. At Rugby, of course, it would have been unthinkable to do other than volunteer as soon as one's age-group was reached. Much time was devoted to the activities of the Training Corps, and competitions between units in the wartime arts were taken almost (but never quite) as seriously as cricket or football matches. Boys who had been prefects only months before came back in well-pressed battledress, with pips on their shoulders and wispy moustaches on their upper lips. The deaths in action of old, and not so old, boys were read out at prayers. It was my good fortune that the war came to an end before my seventeenth birthday, which fell in the autumn of 1945. The end of my schooldays came soon after.

*   *   *   *

For others, conscription continued. Nobody but a masochist, however, would have volunteered in 1946, when thousands of young men were jostling to get themselves demobilised. I was lucky in going straight to Oxford; it was the policy of my college to give an almost absolute priority to ex-servicemen, and only scholars were taken straight from school. So in October 1946, still aged seventeen, I went up to New College, one of a handful of undergraduates of normal age outnumbered by some 400 ex-servicemen. There were many oddities about Oxford life at that period. The college had admitted more undergraduates than could be squeezed into Hall at meal-times. In consequence, the overflow received meal-vouchers to be used in the British Restaurant (a former dance-hall) in the High Street. The waitresses were elderly, flat-footed, and friendly, and meal-times were agreeably flexible, but the food – still rationed of course – was awful. Three ugly prefabricated sets of rooms had been built in the new quad; with their thin partitions, these were not conducive to scholarly peace and quiet. After one term I succeeded in securing a large (though chilly) set of rooms at the summit of the tower, on the pretext that I needed a good north light to engage in experimental painting: there was little competition for these rooms, since only the uncommonly energetic were prepared to face the endless flights of stone stairs that divided living quarters from the bathrooms in the basement.

Most of the undergraduates of that vintage were travelled and experienced warriors in their late twenties; some sported heavy cavalry moustaches, some maintained mistresses, almost all had developed an insatiable thirst for beer. It proved necessary for a seventeen-year-old to grow up very quickly indeed. Of the girls, a rather higher proportion were of my own age group. This stimulating world was very different from Rugby, very different too from home or Blackabbey. I enjoyed myself enormously.

Though I do not think those three years were wasted, I cannot say that I worked very hard; my interests were on the whole extra-mural. I remember principally the beer, the girls, and long summer days spent in punt or canoe on the River Cherwell. I tried my hand at painting pastiches in the styles of the early Flemish and Italian masters; I attended the Slade lectures of Mr Kenneth Clark; I spent a good deal of time looking at the pictures in the Ashmolean; I went often to the theatre, both professional and amateur; I went to occasional concerts in the Music Room in Longwall. But most of my attention was concentrated on poetry. I read it, I wrote it, I talked endlessly about it, and I came to be chairman of the university Poetry Society. This involved giving dinner in the Mitre to the great men who came to read aloud their latest work. Some of these visits were memorable: most of all, the week-end when

Chris Grieve ('Hugh McDiarmid') came down from Glasgow, and his
fare back got spent on drink. He, a fellow-Scot named John Russell, a
fellow-Irishman named Bill McAlpine, Dylan and Caitlin Thomas, and I
spent an uproarious week-end demonstrating the superiority of the
Celtic races combined over the English. At this period Dylan Thomas
was living in a cottage at Witney; each Saturday he would come into
Oxford, and a group of us would meet in the early evening, and then set
out on an exploration of the village pubs in the surrounding countryside.
These pubs, then mostly quite unspoiled, were used by locals only, for
petrol was still rationed. We were dependent for transport on a friendly
printer; five or six of us, including Dylan, would cram ourselves into the
back of his ramshackle van (along with the printer's daughter, and his
large Dalmatian) for the evening. Sometimes a few of us would return to
Witney with Dylan and Bill McAlpine by the last train: once I wheeled
Dylan, curled up in a pram, all the way from Oxford to Witney – in the
guard's van.

The friends I made at Oxford were mostly, however, more nearly of
my own generation. Despite the barrier of the Irish sea, a fair number of
them are friends still. Of my contemporaries, many are now well known
– in the arts, politics, or television, for the most part – but only a few of
these were more than names to me. As an undergraduate I took no active
interest in politics, or in the Union, though some of my friends did so.
Nevertheless, I suppose that a large proportion of the opinions, tastes,
loyalties, and prejudices of a life-time were formed at this time, whether
in the interminable discussions that went on into the small hours, or in
the more casual exchanges that took place in vacations. Two of Naomi
Mitchison's children were friends and contemporaries; it was at this time
that I was first invited to stay with her at Carradale, in the Mull of
Kintyre, only thirty-odd miles across the North Channel from County
Antrim. The conversation in that stimulating household has opened
many windows for me over the years. In 1948 I painted my first mural on
the walls of Carradale; the most recent is less than two years old.
Vacations also gave me my first opportunities to travel: an intoxicating
holiday spent partly in Paris, partly in Savoie, with a group of friends, in
1947; a long summer spent wandering round Italy, for the most part
alone, in 1948.

I sat my history finals in May 1949. As was to be expected in view of
the *train de vie* I had led for the previous three years, I got a mediocre
second. My tutor, Alan Bullock, was disappointed, but I was not much
upset.

*   *   *   *

For many years my father had been tactfully hinting that there would be a place for me in the family firm, if I cared to take it. He exerted no pressure, but I knew how much pleasure it would give him. I left Oxford still undecided; to a young man recently let loose in a larger world, whose interests and ambitions were centred in the arts, the prospect of a lifetime in a dusty office in provincial Belfast was not a very attractive one. I temporised; I told my father that, rather than take the easy course of following the family tramlines, I wished to discover first whether I had the ability to stand on my own feet. I proposed to seek my fortune abroad for a year: concealing his misgivings, he generously agreed. In the late summer of 1949 I set off for Paris to look for a job, with a year's allowance of £25 in my pocket – those were the post-war years of strict foreign-currency control – and a letter of recommendation from Alan Bullock.

I found cheap digs near Montparnasse. After a discouraging fortnight, I fell on my feet: thanks to my tutor's letter, I found a part-time job as a *stagiaire* in the English service of the French Radio. This was a curious organisation with a strongly literary flavour. My ultimate boss was the poet Pierre Emmanuel; below him was Jacques Legris, '*member du tramways Club de Belfast*'; my immediate boss was Daniel Sturge Moore, shaggy, gap-toothed, and exuberant son of the poet Thomas Sturge Moore. We were a tiny, comical team; with a staff of less than a dozen English-speakers, we were expected to produce three hours of programmes each night. My principal task was to write, and then to read, the news bulletins; to select and translate the items that came down from the news room on the top floor of our sleazy offices on the Champs Elysées. An Australian artist and I shared this function under the supervision of an irascible but charming White Russian journalist. But we were expected also to turn our hands to broadcasts of every other kind conceivable; record programmes, quizzes, interviews, literary and artistic criticism, even (once) a running commentary on a football match. When President Sean T. O'Kelly paid a state visit to President Vincent Auriol, I was there, savouring the Dublin French of the one in contrast with the Marseillais accent of the other. I early on endeared myself to our small listening public (mostly English francophiles bored by the correct conventionalism of the BBC) by a spoonerism: instead of announcing that 'Jean Cocteau's cat has won a prize in a cat show', I announced that 'Jean Cateau's cock has won a prize in a cock show'. Though I was reproved, Sturge was really as pleased as the listeners.

I earned at first about £2 a week at the RTF; on this it was just possible to live; it was augmented, but meagrely, by the proceeds of occasional English lessons and translations. I had one meal a day, and that in the subsidised radio canteen, where the menu was always the same: lentil soup, roast horse-meat (which I came to like very well), petits suisses, and a quarter-carafe of a sour blue-purple wine. By degrees I made many friends, both French and foreign. Jean Blaive, in particular, introduced me to the left-wing youth movements of the working-class outer suburbs. I remember with particular pleasure a children's fancy-dress party organised by the anarchists, a very staid body of elderly walrus-whiskered persons. By degrees my financial position improved, and my standard of living rose. After Christmas, I found a part-time teaching job in a school at Mantes, forty miles from Paris. Unusually, this was a Collège Mixte — co-education was then rare in France — but this made the job no easier. I was expected to teach English conversation, without books or teaching aids, to large classes; in the upper forms, both boys and girls were of almost my own age. I soon discovered my shortcomings as a disciplinarian: the girls sat in the front desks and made eyes at me, the boys sat in the back desks and threw chalk at me. The staff was mixed: of my colleagues, two were novelists, Robert Merle and Michel Zeraffa, both now (though not then) well known. We lunched together in the back room of a café in the main street of Mantes. The train journeys to and from the school were disagreeable, but the additional money was welcome. I was able to move to vastly more agreeable digs in the rue des Beaux Arts; my landlady was an elderly but vivacious Russian widow, who kept a pet snail in a colander on her window-ledge, and whose flat (including my room) was exotically furnished with Oriental pieces from Indo-China.

One term of teaching was enough for me: I was lucky to find a far better job, writing the gossip column for the *Continental Daily Mail*. This I shared with a very grand Commander R.N. (retired), *le Commandant* Teddy Phillips. As he was on the closest terms with the Duke and Duchess of Windsor, the Duff Coopers, Nancy Mitford, and so on, he wrote paragraphs about *le-high-life,* and I wrote about *le-low-life.* This division of labour worked admirably, with occasional variations when one of us was otherwise engaged; once in a while I found myself drinking mid-morning champagne at the Travellers', or taking tea with

Mrs Eleanor Roosevelt, or with Sir Duff and Lady Diana at Chantilly.

Columnists in France received two complimentary tickets, not one, from theatre managements and others; and there were plenty of perquisites, including even a week-end at Biarritz for the re-opening of the Casino after the war. Working in the *Mail* office six mornings a week, and in the Radiodiffusion office four evenings a week, with a diverting variety of free social and cultural invitations in between, I was able to support myself more than comfortably. My French was fluent if erratic, my acquaintance was varied and stimulating, I had a perfectly lovely time.

At length, the year drew to an end. It was time to commit myself to a career.

As a bachelor, I had enjoyed spending my twenty-first year in Paris. (My twenty-first birthday had been celebrated, by a coincidence, at a splendid party; the Section Grande-Bretagne had clubbed together to buy a lottery ticket for the Grand Prix de l'Arc de Triomphe; the winnings, worth over £50 — two years' allowance, then! — were all liquidated in our party: I hazily remember reeling home on the pillion of Roland Mehl's motor-bike.) But I had noticed that the young, and less young, married couples of my acquaintance did not seem to have quite so much fun. Did I really want to be a journalist all my life? I looked critically at some of the old soaks who ended their days as reporters or sub-editors on the *Continental Daily Mail*. The answer was definitely No. Did I want to become an editor? I looked affectionately, but quizzically, at my editor, Noel Barber. The answer was still No. Did I aspire to be a Press Baron? I had had a disconcerting passage of arms with my proprietor, Lord Rothermere; I was quite clear that the answer remained an emphatic No. (I was sitting with my feet on my desk, when a large man entered the room without knocking and asked what I was doing; 'Reading the *Continental Daily Mail*', said I; 'Why aren't you writing it?', said he; 'I've written it', said I dismissively. Three minutes later the editor rang down: 'Come to my room, I want you to meet Lord Rothermere'.) My friends thought I must be mad to return to Belfast. I was offered an opening as a foreign correspondent for the Agence France-Presse. Sturge Moore advised me gravely, bless him, on the awful consequences of the choice I faced — between the merry Bohemian life, and the conventional life of a provincial lawyer.

I thought it all over, made up my mind, and returned to Belfast.

EIGHT

I was not the first member of the family to spend an agreeable interlude in Paris; my great-great-great-grandfather Charles Brett saw the city 'to every advantage' in 1790, under the Constituent Assembly, the year of Wordsworth's 'Bliss was it in that dawn to be alive'. Indeed, family legend has it that he was actually present at the fall of the Bastille; in 1874 my great-grandfather wrote to George Benn, the historian of Belfast, 'I have a few fragments of a diary kept by my grandfather giving an account of a journey to France in which, if I recollect aright, he mentions that he was in Paris at the time the Bastile was destroyed'; but as to the truth of this I have my doubts.

The infant Charles Brett, grandson of the bankrupt Bernard, lost his father when he was six; his elder sister Charity having already died in infancy, he was brought up as a fatherless only child by his mother. He addressed a fragment of autobiography to his descendants (only, unfortunately, he got tired half way through). 'Her whole care and sollicitude then centred in me, and she determined to remove from Killough to Belfast, as well to give me the best education, as also to be under the care of the Rev. Bernard Ward, my father's executor and my guardian'. This Mr Ward, a first cousin of Viscount Bangor, was rector of Knockbreda (on the outskirts of Belfast) from 1730 to 1770. He saw to it that the boy was sent to the school in Belfast of David Manson, an enlightened educational theorist far ahead of his time. There he was taught 'English by David Manson: Writing by Carmichael: Dancing by Lee: Music by Rock, a German: French by Eccles: and Classics by the Rev. Mathew Garnet'. In 1765 the Earl and Countess of Donegall paid a visit to their patrimony in Belfast, and received a deputation of schoolboys, when 'Master Brett addressed his Lordship in a Latin oration, to which his Lordship returned an answer in the same language'. (It is to be hoped that his lordship had been forewarned.)

'I was then fit to enter College, but my inclinations being for business, I began to learn the linen trade, which after two unsuccessful trips to Dublin market I grew disgusted with and quit. I then entered into the wine and spirit wholesale business in which I succeeded very well, so that, after some years, I confined myself entirely to the wine trade; in which, as I corresponded with the first houses in Europe (who sent me wines of the very first quality), so I had the first Noblemen and Gentlemen in the north, and even in Dublin, for my customers: by which means my character as a wine merchant grew established and my fortune encreased'. By the age of twenty-one, he had opened a Spirit Cellar in Belfast where he sold the best French brandy, Barbados Rum, Gineva, and, as a side-line, fine white fustian. His ventures prospered amazingly; he was never afraid to diversify the commodities in which he dealt; by 1779, when he was in his late twenties, he was advertising simultaneously brandy, claret, gineva, rum, Old Spirit, red port, madeira, red clover seed, powder blues, fresh pyrmont (whatever that may have been), seltzer water, a few tons of exceeding fine hay, and the letting of a four-acre field near Belfast.

This is all very astonishing in the grandson of a bankrupt Captain of militia. Where did he obtain his capital? Where did this commercial talent spring from? But there can be no doubt of it: Charles Brett was one of the first of the new Whig merchant class that sprang up in Ireland in the second half of the eighteenth century. He was, I think, not a likeable young man; spoiled, brash, and aggressive; the local gossip, Mrs McTier, remarked some ten years later 'Chas Brett is not loved'. But that he was energetic and talented cannot be denied: he displayed already many of the qualities for which, in the years of the Industrial Revolution and the High Victorian period, Belfast was to become noted.

His business interests, throughout his life, were multifarious. He was involved in a local, and unsuccessful, distillery; and was a shareholder in the Belfast Glassworks, also unsuccessful. He acted as land agent for Lord Yelverton's Ballymacarrett estate near Belfast, and as a house agent. He was for several years secretary to the Belfast Annuity Company, an interesting venture half-way between a friendly society and a modern insurance company, which collapsed in 1795. He was a founder member, in 1783, of the Belfast Chamber of Commerce, and one of the signatories two years later to a petition opposing Pitt's Twenty Propositions on Anglo-Irish Trade. He dealt in 'whalebone of the very best quality for the use of staymakers and whipmakers'. He farmed, and grew flax, and experimented with new methods of retting it. And in his later years he was active in a local merchant-adventuring concern, which owned at one time eight brigs trading around the British Isles. This was a very high-risk business: in January 1815 he wrote to his son Wills, 'The Levant: Capt. McKibbin: and who, with a most valuable cargo going to London, was given up for lost; has got into Milford Haven, after having been blown about in the channel and into the Western Ocean for 31 days, and were obliged to throw all their guns and water casks overboard, by which means they had no water for ten days but what they caught in their sails: Mr Greenlaw was so sure he was gone that he sent over to London to purchase another ship. Poor Archy McMullan was in her, and if you had seen old Marg's face when I took her the account that the Levant was safe, you would have enjoyed it highly'. Charles Brett clearly became more amiable as he grew older.

His visit to revolutionary Paris was brought about by another high-risk investment:

I was induced to take a share in an adventure to New Orleans thro' the persuasion of an old schoolfellow, James Trail Kennedy, under the guidance of his cousin, James Kennedy, who betrayed the trust reposed in him so egregiously, and acted the rogue so compleatly, that all the parties concerned here, and Messrs. V. and P. French of Bordeaux, would have been involved in great loss and difficulties: if I had not, at the request of the other partners, gone over to that city in a passage from Bangor Quay to the city of Bordeaux of only 96 hours. There, after first seizing our ship, fraudulently sold by Kennedy, I settled all the accounts of the concern with the Messrs. French, so as not only to overthrow a claim to a large amount they had furnished against the partners here: but brought a balance in our favour which was settled and paid by bills on London.
Whilst in Bordeaux I was strongly invited by two great Houses to go into a share of their establishment, as also to form a matrimonial connection with a very beautiful young lady, since married to a peer of high rank in England; but as she was a Roman Catholic, and I saw bad times coming on the country, I declined both offers, and returned home by Paris and London: after settling the business which took me out in the most satisfactory manner, gaining high respect and friendship from many persons, and knowledge in the wine trade; and having a most delightful opportunity of travelling through France and England and seeing Paris and London to every advantage.

How characteristic of the Ulster business-man is the self-abnegation involved in refusing to marry a 'very beautiful young lady', ward to a great wine shipper, because of her religious persuasion! Despite this act of prudence however, and despite the strongly Anglican piety he was to display in later years when his son took holy orders, Charles Brett was by no means an anti-Catholic bigot. He had been one of the earliest members of 'The Belfast Company Associated for learning the Military Exercises', predecessor of the Irish Volunteer movement. Indeed, in 1778 he allowed his name to go forward for election to the post of Second Lieutenant; but in the democratic ballot, he received only one vote (one hopes not his own). And at a large meeting of Belfast citizens, held in January 1792, he voted for a resolution 'That our Roman Catholic brethren have long been, and still are, in a degraded situation from numerous restrictive and penal statutes hanging over them; and conscious as we are, that the prosperity, happiness and improvement of this country must eventually depend on an union of interests among all religious denominations of the inhabitants — we therefore pray the legislature may be pleased to repeal all penal and restrictive statutes at present in existence against the Roman Catholics of Ireland'. It must in honesty be added, however, that he was one of the 255 citizens who supported an amendment (outvoted by a very large majority: what a sizeable meeting it must have been) desiring to defer this step until 'the circumstances of the country, and the welfare of the whole kingdom will permit'. He was an admirer of Grattan and Curran, and in 1809 presented the speeches of the latter to his eleven-year-old son 'as a Model well worthy of his Imitation'.

Rather surprisingly, Charles Brett abandoned the family tradition of dependence on the Ward family, and offered his political allegiance to Lord Downshire. (In much later correspondence with Lord Down-shire, in 1823, Charles Brett asserted that there had been a friendly relationship between the two families for over a century: which takes us back to Bernard Brett.) It is not clear whether he was active in the contested Down election of 1790, when Arther Hill (later 2nd Marquis of Downshire), Robert Stewart (later Lord Castlereagh), and Richard Ward (younger son of Viscount Bangor) were three of the four candidates for the two county seats. But there is some evidence that he was, and in opposition to the Ward candidate. In this election, Ward and Stewart stood for parliamentary reform on Whig principles, Hill and Matthews for the then establishment. But the tables were turned soon after, when Stewart was the author of the Act of Union, and the Hill family stood for the independence of the Irish Parliament. The support given by Charles Brett to the Downshire party was almost certainly at the suggestion of John (commonly known as Jack) Brett of Downpatrick. When Charles Brett's father had died in 1758, his cousin Matthew had succeeded to the Ward agency in Killough; Matthew's son, also a solicitor, had become one of Lord Downshire's land agents, and as a Downshire protégé ultimately became County Treasurer, and a very rich man. Jack Brett was a convivial fellow, and a confirmed bachelor. 'He drank largely of wine for many years of his later life, and in the evenings often made himself ridiculous. He is supposed never to have had commerce with the other sex. He was of middle stature, but very light frame, hair almost white in his age, snuffed to excess, was generally healthy, and died very suddenly upon the roadside in the country, when out in his carriage for exercise'. It seems likely that Jack Brett gave a helping hand to his much younger cousin Charles, perhaps by lending him capital for his early adventures into commerce, almost certainly by introducing him to Lord Downshire and enlisting him amongst the 'clients' (in the Roman sense) of the latter.

It was through Lord Downshire's influence that in January 1797 Charles Brett was appointed to the lucrative but onerous post of barrack-master of Belfast, a position he was to hold during the rising of 1798 and throughout the Napoleonic wars. It seems not to have had the political overtones that would now attach to such a position. The previous holder of the post, Arthur Bunting, was seriously ill, and Mrs McTier (who had been trying to get the job for her husband Sam) wrote to Dr Drennan that the employment was given by Government 'past Lord Donegall to the Marquis of Downshire's friend, on condition that £200 and one year's profit, supposed to be £500, should be paid to the Miss Buntins, which is to be done by Charly Brett of Charleville, for having been coffined at the last election – Downshire never forgets his friends, in that and other things also he has much the advantage of Londonderry'. To be 'coffined' meant to be the recipient of a death-threat; these anonymous threats took the form of a plain unsigned sheet of paper, the name of the person threatened being written inside a coffin-shaped surround – a form of intimidation not unknown in the 1970s.

Indeed the years leading up to the rising of '98 were very troubled ones, offering many lamentable comparisons with the present day. The Secret Committee of the Irish Parliament later reported 'In the latter end of 1796, and the beginning of 1797, the loyal inhabitants of Ulster suffered most severely from the depradations of the United Irishmen; throughout the province they were stript of their arms; the most horrid murders were perpetrated by large bodies of men in open day, and it became nearly impossible to bring the offenders to justice from the inevitable destruction that awaited the witnesses or jurors who dared to perform their duty'. Exactly the same problem faces the authorities still; the most successful expedient used to surmount it has been the confidential telephone. Early in 1797 Charles Brett was one of a group of twelve County Down gentlemen who endeavoured to set up an equivalent system: each subscribed to a fund out of which rewards were to be paid to those who should give confidential information – 'and we solemnly pledge ourselves that we will keep the names of such persons professionally secret' – as to the authors of outrages, and in particular those 'forcibly entering houses at night, sometimes with blackened faces, robbing the inhabitants of their arms, and murdering such as have been active in endeavouring to preserve peace and suppress insurrection'.

When it erupted, in May and June 1798, the rising came close to repeating the events of 1688. It broke out first in Wexford, then in County Antrim, a few days later in County Down. Vast numbers of refugees fled, as in 1688, to Stranraer, the Isle of Man, Lancashire, and Wales. Donaghadee, the normal mail station for cross-channel shipping, was taken by the United Irishmen, as was the whole of the Ards peninsula and the greater part of North Down. The troops available were perhaps sufficient to deal with the rising in each of the two northern counties separately, but quite insufficient to deal with both at once. On Sunday 10 June (known later as 'Pike Sunday') one James McKey, a tide-waiter or junior employee in the excise, wrote an agitated letter to Lord Downshire describing the position: interestingly, his letter was counter-signed by Charles Brett and Captain MacNevin, the barrack-masters respectively of Belfast and Carrickfergus:

Never was a place in such confusion as this town and neighbourhood at this instant. – The rebels have broke out with uncommon violence in the County of Down. Saintfield, Newtown, Comber & the whole of that country is in their possession & I am sorry to tell you they have drove off every force could be sent, & all have retreated, yeomen etc., etc, to this town, with several detachments from this Garrison that was sent out to their relief. In short my lord we want force sufficient, & we are told there is seven regiments at Portpatrick ready to come but dare not venture by Donaghadee. Coming by Carrickfergus will add delay, & god send it may be not too long. . . . Our troops here are up day &

night & I write this long side my horse on guard. . . . Almost all the females of this town are set out for Scotland by Carrickfergus today, as it is thought this town will be attacked. Twenty yeomen got possession of the Market House in Newton, and have done great execution, think of the state General Nugent must be in, when he cannot send them relief. . . . Big Birch came here a few hours ago with part of the Newton cavalry, & a man so much frightened I never saw. . . . Tomorrow something (or this night) must be done.

Finally, in his excitement McKey so far forgot himself as to sign his letter to the Marquis simply 'ever yours'!

In the event, General Nugent succeeded in defeating the United Irishmen at Ballynahinch three days later, without having received reinforcements from Scotland or elsewhere. By concentrating the small force at his disposal first against the County Antrim men, and then (almost without a pause for rest) against those of County Down, leaving Belfast practically undefended meanwhile, he ended the rising once and for all. Probably the United Irishmen could not have won in any event without the hoped-for landing of French troops; but if the risings in Wexford, Kildare, Antrim, and Down had been better co-ordinated, they might well have taken the north-eastern counties, as in 1688, and held them at least until the arrival of reinforcements from England. That they failed was partly due to the collapse of the somewhat shaky alliance between Catholics and Presbyterians in the United Irishmen's ranks. Already, on 4 June, Lord Downshire's agent in Hillsborough was able to report:

We have been much alarmed these ten days past at the situation of affairs in the south — it turns out to be a religious contest, the accounts of the ravages committed by the insurgents exceed belief — it is said that at Enniscorthy every Protestant man woman & child, even infants, have been murdered, a second St Bartholomew is dreaded. . . . Tho' these deluded rebels have been the cause of the death of many innocent & loyal people, there is one effect that appears to have derived from it & made a rapid progress — it has detached the Protestants from a union with them in their treasonable views — their eyes are now opened.

Family tradition has it that Charles Brett's infant son Wills, born in January 1798, was hidden by his nursemaid in a ditch near Charleville for fear the rebels might come that way after the Battle of Ballynahinch; as well they might have done, for a great part of the barony of Castlereagh was in their hands.

In 1790 Charles Brett owned a large town house in the High Street of Belfast (from which 'some audacious person' in that year burgled the family knives and forks, 'with my crest upon them, a faulcon'); and he also took on long lease from Lord Downshire a farm of 26 acres at Castlereagh. Here he built a comfortable house, which he called Charleville: at first he used it mainly as a summer residence, but after his semi-retirement it became his home all the year round. The house is still standing, though much altered during the Victorian period. Both the house and garden, and especially the romantic glen near by, in a pleasant hollow of the Castlereagh hills a few miles from Belfast, retain something of their original rural character. In November 1795 Charles Brett's mother died, and only three weeks later he married in Dublin Matilda Black, daughter of a family of merchants in Armagh. Mrs McTier wrote cattily to her brother, 'Chas Britt goes up to be married to a fair Black with fifteen hundred'. He was then forty-three, she thirty. It was a very happy marriage: seven children were born of it, of whom three (two of them named Charles) were to die in infancy. The eldest, Matilda, was named after her mother. The eldest son was named Wills Hill after the 1st Marquis of Downshire; the youngest daughter was called Mary Catherine Sandys after the wife of the 2nd Marquis of Downshire; the survivor of the twins born in 1800 was Anna Bella.

The family was a musical one; Charles Brett himself played the violin and guitar; he was a close friend of Edward Bunting, who first collected the airs of the surviving harpers; and to Charleville the harpers were bidden to celebrate his birthdays. Matilda, 'a musical lass', was a good amateur singer. Mary and Matilda junior played the piano forte: the house contained an upright piano by Stodard, and a Broadwood grand piano. In 1816 Charles Brett wrote: 'I sold the old piano forte, and have not got another yet from London, but daily look for it: it will I have no doubt be as good as possible of the kind: a square one: as I know Stodart the maker will exert himself for me'. It will be remembered how large the gift of a Broadwood piano from Frank Churchill to Jane Fairfax loomed in the plot of *Emma,* published in the same year. The girls took singing lessons from Signor Guarini. Books and gardening were other interests: also furnishing and decoration: in 1814 the family spent the winter at Charleville, and Anna Bella wrote to her sister at boarding school, 'Mr Gillis returned from France and has brought from thence the most beautiful room paper I ever saw, it is a view of the Isle of Elba, representing on one side sea, shipping and docks, on the other, old castles, planting and people. It is put on the round room and when you are sitting in it you almost think you are in the open air'.

The family was distinctly pious in a conventional, Church of Ireland, sort of way. Charles Brett personally was an active member of the building committee responsible for the erection of St George's church (originally just 'George's church', so named in honour of King George III, not the patron saint of England), in the High Street, Belfast, to the designs of the Dublin architect John Bowden, but re-using the splendid portico originally erected at Ballyscullion by the Earl-bishop of Derry. In his later years he attended Newtonbreda church, where he must have gone as a boy when his guardian Bernard Ward was rector. He and Lord Deramore, who lived at Belvoir, were not on friendly terms, and both claimed the same pew. Matters came to such a pass that Lord Deramore had the door of the disputed pew padlocked; on discovering this one Sunday, Charles Brett instantly fetched the blacksmith from the village and had the lock struck off in time for service. He was much given to charitable works, and during one hard winter, advertised an open invitation to anyone who was hungry to take Sunday lunch with him at Charleville: I would dearly like to know what happened, but the advertisement was not repeated. He wrote helpful letters also to the Belfast papers advising local employers to buy in large stocks of fuel, clothing, and so forth at wholesale discounts, and resell them to their servants and labourers at cost, in order to raise the standards of living of the latter.

The elder girls were educated at home, but Wills was sent to Trinity College, Dublin, in 1813, and Mary, the youngest, was sent away to boarding school at Avenham in Lancashire at the very early age of eleven. Their mother was by then in poor health, and the letters to and from school betray some anxiety, as well as some rather forced cheerfulness. In a letter to her father in April 1815 Mary makes the puzzling remark, 'I think your comparison of my dear mother to a pineapple plant is but too just'. A month later there was a suggestion of a family visit to Mary at school, but nothing came of it; in May, just after the escape from Elba, just a month before Waterloo, Matilda wrote to her daughter: 'I want to guard you against being too sanguine of seeing us this summer, as I don't think it is at all likely, your father finds so much to do in his Barrack department owing to the probability of a fresh war breaking out immediately, that he is almost sure he cannot be spared so long from his post . . . we must only vent our disappointment on *Boneparte*'. The family did not go over, and Mary did not come home, that summer; she was in fact never to see her mother again; for Matilda died aged forty-nine in October 1815.

The duties of barrack-master must, indeed, have been quite onerous during the years between 1798 and 1815; despite the calls for troops elsewhere, a substantial garrison was maintained in Ireland throughout the Napoleonic wars. The general quarter-mastering administration was carried on from Dublin, but Charles Brett was responsible for the stores, fodder, repairs, and upkeep of a quite extensive series of buildings – in 1814 he advertised for tenders for the whitewashing of 'the Officers' and Privates' Rooms, Stair-Cases, Galleries, Guard-Houses, and Necessaries of the Old and New Barracks of Belfast; as also the two Regimental Hospitals, in Barrack and Carrickfergus-Streets; and also the Joints of the Bedsteads in said Barracks and Hospitals'. It is not clear how he was remunerated: a circular from Dublin inquiring what allowances he had received as a half-pay officer holding a barrack-mastership is endorsed 'Answer, never, I had received none'.

The ending of the war in 1814 was received with great rejoicing, and 'a very general illumination in the town and parish of Castlereagh. There were some very beautiful transparencies. . . . Bonfires blazed on every hill, and much rejoicing till a late hour; and although there were many touched with the native, yet, much to the honour of the place, all was peace' – so the *Belfast News Letter* reported. Charles Brett's prosperity had suffered considerable reverses during the long-drawn-out Napoleonic wars, especially in consequence of the Continental blockade. He was very conscious of the expense of sending his children away to be educated. In 1814 he wrote to Wills in Dublin explaining his inability to increase his allowance owing to a present shortage of cash: 'and therefore, I don't see how the new coat or hat is to come either to you or to me . . . all I can say by way of comfort is that I am going on Wednesday to wait on the Marquis of Downshire, & it will be in the old blue coat and same hat you left me with here: I don't mean the chip one, as that would raise an uproar in the house I could never stand'. A year later, he tells Mary he is sending a remittance to Mrs Godfrey, her schoolma'am, which, as well as those 'for Wills at College (& which are not light) I pay with the greatest pleasure: because I am sure I will get *value received*'. And to Wills in 1815, in a letter largely concerned with money matters and his conduct at college (which was fortunately 'gentlemanly') – 'here I sit acquit to my God and my conscience: of evincing my fatherly care to you all in a manner, which few: very few: parents in my Moderate Circumstances would ever have thought of, much less attempted'.

All his life Charles Brett enjoyed making lavish use of the advertising columns of the local press; in 1824, aged seventy-two, he decided to retire for good to Charleville, and offered for sale or to let his 'excellent pew, in the west gallery, George's church, with cushions complete'; and also the shop and house in High Street. (The latter eventually became William Doig's timber-store, and was finally destroyed by I.R.A. bombs in 1970.) Another advertisement was to appear in 1826 under the heading Stop Thief: 'Owen M'Aleer, a stable boy in my service, ran away on Tuesday morning . . . and took away a servant's light drab surtout, with white metal buttons, a blue coat with gilt buttons, and a castor hat, all which articles were nearly new; all my property; he was guilty of many acts of swindling and raising money under false pretences. He was a thief, and a confirmed drunkard'.

In his will, which he made in 1827, another more satisfactory servant was remembered: 'to my old and faithful servant Alexander Reed such part or proportion of my Hats Shirts and Cravats Stockings Shoes and wearing apparel as my son shall judge proper . . . and the long sea chest to keep them in, also my silver watch by Tom McCabe; and I desire all my children to be kind and good to him (as I have been) and to allow him as long as he lives in his service and behaves himself as he ought (of which my son is to be the sole judge) the annual sum of five pounds a year; . . . but shall he misbehave (which I trust for his own sake he will not) . . . any further payment is to cease; but go when he may, the cloaths, chest and watch are to be his'.

The will is very long, mingling legal verbosity with Charles Brett's own expansive style. Wills was executor and residuary legatee; each of the girls was left £1,500 and some rents. There are long and detailed lists of belongings: Matilda was to get the upright piano and her mother's gold watch; Anna Bella 'the minature picture of her dear mother whom she so much resembles in sweetness of disposition', the low gig and black mare Bet to draw it, 'my two guitars and violin', and many miscellaneous house furnishings; Mary the Broadwood grand, 'which she so well deserves as a tribute to the pleasure she so often afforded her dear Father by the masterly way she played on it', the young black mare (out of Bet) and side saddle, furniture and effects,

The Whole Duty of Man, Wilson's Sacrament, the *Spectators* and *Guardians,* and *Thomson's Seasons.* Each of the girls was left £10 'to purchase decent mourning for her father who loved her'.

In fact, Charles Brett lived for another two years and died at the age of seventy-seven on 23 June 1829. I am sure he would have wished me to end this chapter, as he ended his own will, with a breathless roll of drums by way of exordium:

And now having made this distribution of my wordly property to the very best of my judgement In addition to that I bequeath to my dear and beloved children my last and parental blessing in sure and certain hope that as they have all deserved it from me their Father it will bring down GODS blessing on them and their Posterity and let them always keep in remembrance and follow the example they received from their dear Mother which uniformly afforded me the most perfect happiness this world could afford and above all things (next to the love of God) let them love one another as their dear Father loved them not as too frequent in this World as long as the sunshine of prosperity lasts but in all situations (however arduous which may occur to any of them either by decay of health or fortune) let them redouble and exert their love and affection to each other the sure hope of which will make me Die in Peace and haveing therefore bequethed my Body to the Dust from whence it came nothing remains but to recommend my soul to that GOD who gave it through the infinite mercies of our blessed Lord Saviour and Redeemer JESUS CHRIST.

NINE

Although Belfast has been the family home since young Charles Brett was brought there by his newly widowed mother, for the benefit of his education, in 1758, I myself hardly knew the city at all until I was in my twenties. My boyhood was mostly spent in outer-suburban County Down, when I was not away at school or university. To me, Belfast meant visits to have my hair cut, and to exchange dreary coupons for dreary clothes; visits to my three great-aunts on the Malone Road; visits to see a ship launched at the Queen's Island – an entertainment in which a large part of the population of Belfast always participated; and visits to my father's office on the way back from Blackabbey.

For a few months after my return to Ulster I lived with my parents, but it soon became plain that I was likely to make only 'suitable' friends in this way, and that was far from my intention. For most of the three-year span of my apprenticeship I lived in a bed-sitter flat in East Belfast, on the rise overlooking the shipyards and the rows of small houses of Ballymacarrett, my Sunday slumbers disturbed by the bells of Butterfield's St Mark's, Dundela, just across the road. My apprenticeship itself, though the exams were tedious, was enjoyable. On some afternoons I attended lectures at the Queen's University, or at the Law Society. But most of the time was spent working with, or for, my father – and this close relationship between father and son I enjoyed as much as I have enjoyed anything in my life – or in gossiping about clients, past and present, with Dick McCausland, the managing clerk.

I was not much interested in the theory of the law. But I was deeply interested in the endless succession of conundrums, some human, some procedural, that the clients came to have resolved. Some were as complex as cats' cradles. Sometimes the solutions come out more quickly and easily, though, if the solicitor already knows the ins and outs of the client's background or family history. I found it fascinating to watch how, from the records and recollections of the generations within the firm, illuminating facts (sometimes surprising, sometimes shocking) would be brought into play. Numerous and entertaining were the intimate life-histories of clients; my father or Dick McCausland knew most of them. But if they should be gravelled, all three of us would turn to my grandfather, still attending the office daily though nearly ninety. His eyes would light up; he would pass a hand over his beautifully brushed head of white hair; he would put on (or take off) his spectacles; and in measured and well-chosen words would tell us exactly how it came about that Mr So-and-So had been born on the wrong side of Mrs Somebody's blanket.

At this period the office building had become very dingy. It was still lit, and for the most part heated, by gas. There was a coal fire in my father's (now my) room: he sat on (what is now) my side of the desk, my grandfather on the far side. The outer office contained an iron cage, with a mahogany-panelled cubicle; by means of this contrivance the waiting clients could sit in privacy and warmth beside the gas fire, while some of the warmth passed between the bars of the cage to Miss Darragh and Miss Hamilton. The office-boy (there were still office-boys then) shared with the court clerk a small room in the return, known as the Despatch, which contained a letter-press, from which dark-purple copies of type-written letters were squeezed, like wine from grapes, into fat copy-books. The basement was the territory of Robert Boyd, the caretaker, though his kitchen fire and chair were available for lady typists who felt unwell, or clients overcome by the cold. Lord Craigavon, I was told, had remained a faithful client despite my great-grandfather's Liberal politics; he used to walk into the city from Strandtown, and, before consulting his solicitor, would always go downstairs to the basement and dry his socks before the caretaker's fire – he was still remembered by the older members of the staff, not for his premiership, but for the smelliness of his feet. Upstairs, the back office (formerly Mr L'Estrange's) was shared between an elderly salaried solicitor whom my father had taken on after the war, a younger solicitor, and me. The former front drawing-room was divided into three cubicles by tall mahogany desks, screens, and high stools; here sat Dick McCausland and his secretary, Miss Kenny; here also sat the elderly and crotchety book-keeper, Mrs Hall, of whom I went in fear. On the floor above were the costs-drawer, Mr Smith, and his acolyte; and three typists. Above this again were attics full of old ledgers, and a room known as the Committee Room, in which it had been great-grandfather's custom to eat an egg for lunch – the egg having been boiled for him by the apprentice, my father. And above this again, in the roof-space, were further attics full of the musty documents of a century and more – though these had been thinned out in 1940 for fear of incendiary bombs.

In these archaic arrangements I proposed a number of changes, some of which I now regret. The office was in 1950 a late-Victorian survival, of a kind then already rare, now quite disappeared. There was, however (not to overstate the case), room for some modernisation. And, looking back, I marvel at the tolerance with which the brash reforms of a 22-year-old were accepted. For it was still then, what is barely conceivable today, an old-fashioned family firm; and provided Mr Alfred and Mr Charlie gave the word, young Master Charles (as Dick McCausland and Jack Smith could not be dissuaded from calling me) could do no wrong.

*   *   *   *

Although I had previously taken no great interest in politics, I had decided, before returning to Ulster, that I ought no longer to stand aside. I was clear that my sympathies were overwhelmingly on the side of those less privileged than I had been. In general I strongly approved of the policies of the post-war Labour government under Attlee. Though a radical and a reformer at heart, yet I was not a theoretical socialist. I had no more interest in political theory than in the theory of law; it was the human and practical side of politics that interested me. I felt that the working people of Ulster would benefit from fuller parity with the welfare state as understood in Labour Britain: so that the traditions of Irish nationalism and republicanism did not attract me. On the contrary, I felt myself to be very much a European and an internationalist. I was therefore left with a straightforward choice: as many people then and later advised me to do, I could join the deeply entrenched Unionist party, and endeavour to lever it leftward from inside; or I could join the tiny and feeble Northern Ireland Labour Party. The former alternative held out some possibilities of success, and every prospect of political promotion to a position of power; that is, the power enjoyed by a big fish in a small pool. The latter alternative was almost quixotic in practical terms, certainly in the short run, but it was honourable, straightforward, and challenging. Moreover, the smugness and self-satisfaction of Unionists at all levels, and the overbearing way in which they then ran their one-party state, would seem today almost unbelievable; so that it appeared a positive public duty to stand outside and bung bricks at them: a duty that I performed to the best of my ability, and with relish, for the next twenty years.

Very soon after my return to Belfast, I went to call on the secretary of the Labour Party, Sam Napier. I found a plump and cheerful young man in a natty bow tie, only a few years older than I, who was to become an intimate ally and a lifelong friend. Since there was no branch near my parents' home, he directed me to the East Belfast branch of the Labour Party, and there I presented myself for the first time on a November evening in 1950. There were present some thirty-odd people, of all age groups, drawn from a variety of craft and working-class backgrounds, for the most part connected in one way or another with the shipyard and Shorts' aircraft factory. At that period the party had very few middle-class members. Members addressed each other as 'comrade', and the chair as 'comrade chairman', and for the first time I experienced the discipline of debate conducted strictly in accordance with the rules of order laid down in Sir Walter Citrine's *ABC of Chairmanship*, the bible of Labour and Trade Union branches. I cannot now remember what was the subject-matter of the discussion that night, but it was fiery, passionate, articulate, and embraced an intriguing interplay between idealism and personality. I was hooked. After the meeting, I found that I had missed the last bus home; David and Winnie Bleakley kindly invited me to spend the night with them in the their house near by. Most of the night was spent talking: I had crossed the threshold into a new world, in which I was soon to make myself much at home, and to make many new friends.

When I arrived at the office after my night out, it was to find that my mother had sent me (via my father) clean socks, hankie, shirt, and collar, with a cryptic and rather uncharacteristic message, expressing the hope 'that she had been nice'!

*   *   *   *

Quickly I was drawn into the activities of the Labour Party. My experience as a journalist, modest as it was, led me to the drafting of press statements and, later, policy documents. I prepared election addresses and leaflets, and saw to their layout and printing. I was given the task of editing (which meant largely writing) the party's journal, named with inappropriate optimism *The Rising Tide* (also the name of a dockside pub in East Belfast, as ribald commentators pointed out). I learned the art of canvassing from house to house at election times, an art I particularly enjoyed: I liked meeting and talking to people on their doorsteps; I liked being asked indoors for an argument. Over the years I must have canvassed at least half of the streets of Belfast, which is a large city. Not only did I come to know the geography and characteristics of different parts of the city, I came to grasp some of the infinitely subtle nuances that distinguished the ways of life of the parallel but quite separate class hierarchies of Catholic and Protestant families, from the upper crust to the down and out.

My new colleagues for the most part made me very welcome. There were a few old stagers, adherents of the theory of class warfare, who treated me with cool suspicion. But the majority of members, though a bit surprised, were pleased to welcome to the ranks an energetic young man from a legal family with a Rugby, Oxford, and Paris background. And here I found that my great-grandfather's reputation as a leading local Liberal stood me in good stead. Very early on, Tom Boyd, pattern-maker and later leader of the Parliamentary Party at Stormont, introduced me to his mother: she greeted me very warmly; the family had always been a radical one, and she recalled her father saying that, if any of them should be in trouble, 'ye may gan till Charlie Brett'.

The reaction of many, though happily by no means all, of the conventional Unionists I met in the way of business was very different. Some of them were quite remarkably unpleasant. I was sometimes called to my face a 'traitor to my class', and a 'traitor to my family' – those who called me the latter being unfamiliar with the family history. The 'Border Election' of 1949 was still close in time. The British Labour Party was deeply distrusted as having anti-partitionist sympathies. To be anything but Unionist was regarded as treacherously disloyal in anyone of Protestant upbringing, though of course only to be expected in a Catholic. The middle and professional classes were at this time more intolerant than the working class; as a canvasser, I had things actually thrown at me only twice in the red-hot Protestant areas (once in Island Street, once in Memel Street). My grandfather became alarmed at the possible effects of my politics on the firm. He had been through all this before: he had seen the clients wincing at my great-grandfather's Home Rule politics. My father too was uneasy, though he stood up for my right to hold and express my own opinions. In the end a compromise was hammered out: I was to be free to engage in politics as I wished, so long as I did not stand for any public office. It was not an entirely satisfactory arrangement, but it suited well enough in the end. I certainly wanted to be a solicitor more than I wanted to be a politician. And it removed from me the temptations of personal ambition in the political field – no small advantage in that quarrelsome world where personalities loom so large.

*   *   *   *

Two years before my homecoming, on one of my country pub-crawls with Dylan Thomas, I had met a BBC producer from Belfast, John Boyd. He asked me to look him up on my return; when I did so, I found that my experience with Radiodiffusion Française could be put to good use in Belfast. As a result of a number of 'talks' programmes, I obtained the entry to a quite different world within Belfast: that of the arts. This was of unexpected richness. Not, to be truthful, in terms of creative production; apart from expatriate Ulstermen such as Louis MacNeice, Tyrone Guthrie, and Bertie Rodgers, there were then few if any local practitioners of any of the arts who aspired to the first rank. But the talk was good. There were intersecting intellectual circles, each informed, witty, and amusing in its own way, centred on rival public-houses, semi-professional theatres, and clubs. These drew both strength and vigour from the contrasting strands of Catholic and Protestant culture running through the community. (This same interaction of traditions has contributed largely to the surprising artistic flowering that has accompanied the most recent Troubles.) The worlds of the arts, and of trade unionism – the two fields in which I sought and found most of my friends – were, as it happened, the only two fields of Ulster life from which sectarianism was wholly absent; in each, Catholic and Protestant could mix quite naturally and unself-consciously as they could do almost nowhere else.

Having no interest in sports of any kind, I was not attracted by the world of football clubs, tennis clubs, yacht clubs, and golf clubs to which most of my middle-class contemporaries belonged. Like my great-grandfather, I have a particular dislike of golf, the most wasteful land-use in the world; I have long advocated the establishment of Government Retraining Schools for teaching golfers chess. Nor was I attracted by the world of those whom Brendan Behan dubbed the 'Horse Protestants', the way of life so popular in Ireland revolving around hunting, racing, and point-to-points. Shooting or fishing might have attracted me, and indeed I had been taken out to shoot grouse and snipe when I was younger, and had enjoyed it; but by degrees I had come to have a disinclination – I put it no more strongly than that – for the unnecessary taking of life. I must ruefully admit to having a very highly developed capacity for disapproving of things that other people enjoy. (I even manage to disapprove of umbrellas: being a tall man, I have a phobia that a dear little old lady, scurrying by with her head down, will one day gouge one of my eyes out with the end of one of the steel ribs of her umbrella.) It is perhaps as well that I never sought a career in politics: a candidate who managed to disapprove at the same time of all forms of organised sport and of all forms of organised religion could expect to antagonise a large majority, if not two large majorities, of his electors. Perhaps I was, or am, an intellectual snob, or a prig, or both; 'don't be so austere, Charlie! have another bottle of stout!' was the constant cry of my friend James Boyce; but at least I manage to approve of wine, women, song, and the arts.

To that bohemian life James Boyce certainly belonged. I first met him on St Patrick's day of 1951, and until his death, he was the closest friend I had. He was then a school-master, shortly to throw up his safe but stifling job for the perilous life of a freelance broadcaster. His house in University Street was a meeting place for people of the most diverse interests and talents, where conversation and all the ephemeral arts flourished. There and at various literary and journalistic pubs, it was possible to meet interesting people who by no means belonged to the conventional Unionist world: established actors, authors, playwrights, and painters: but also, odd men out such as Sam Thompson, shipyard playwright; Markey Robinson, boilermaker turned artist; George McCann, at once military man and sculptor; Fiddler Moore, tram-conductor turned linguist and entertainer; Ralph Bossence, newspaper columnist and glass-in-hand-philosopher.

I had apprehensively feared to find Belfast a black, boring, provincial city, and life there a dreary come-down after Oxford and Paris. I was quite wrong: below the grimy and conventional surface, it was a city bursting with a stimulating life of its own, fed by the conflicts hidden not far below the surface. No doubt, from the plateau of middle age, or the trough of the continuing Troubles, I tend to look back to some extent to a lost golden age; but I still think that in the 1950s and 60s life in Belfast was probably more invigorating and rewarding than in Dublin, Glasgow, or any other provincial city of the British Isles.

*　　　*　　　*　　　*

If I have too light-heartedly given the impression that life was all pubs, booze, and talk, this is far from true. Outside politics and the law, there were other exacting and sometimes rewarding activities. In 1954, in the teeth of opposition from within the BBC establishment, John Boyd embarked upon a series of radio programmes designed to open up the current affairs of Ulster to public discussion between Protestants and Catholics. The series was based on the English 'Any Questions' programmes, then extremely popular. A team of four performers and a chairman travelled round the towns and villages of Ulster, and gave spontaneous answers to questions from the floor. The basic team consisted of Desmond Neill, a Quaker sociologist, as chairman; Jack Sayers, editor of the *Belfast Telegraph* and an unusually liberal Unionist; J. J. Campbell, lecturer in St Mary's Catholic Teacher Training College; Jim Beckett, Professor of Irish History at Queen's University; and myself. Sometimes local politicians were invited to take part, sometimes distinguished performers from across the water, such as Professor Bronowski and Mary Stocks. Between 1954 and 1965 160 editions of the programme were broadcast: it was eventually overtaken by television. During those ten years it had, I believe, a considerable effect in relaxing the old sectarian tensions and subjecting to reasoned (and good-mannered) argument the attitudes and activities of nationalists and unionists alike.

Gradually, during this period, as an experienced broadcaster I had come to be one of the principal public spokesmen for the Labour Party. When television arrived, I was obliged to conform to its new restraints, though I still preferred (as I still prefer) sound radio, both as performer and as consumer (except when they play cricket instead of music on Radio Three). The grounding in techniques I had received in Paris stood me in good stead. I took part in many confrontation programmes with politicians of other parties, and especially Unionist ministers, some of whom were nonentities whose bigotry was their only passport to success. Perhaps I am swollen-headed in retrospect, but I still think that these confrontations had a useful influence on public opinion; and that if O'Neill had had the courage to concede reforms before it was too late majority opinion would have supported him. But the effects of reasoned argument on the television audience came to an end when, instead, viewers were treated to film of riot, stone-throwing, tear-gas, fire, and explosion. Such images had, and still have, more effect than any amount of reasoned argument.

LONG SHADOWS CAST BEFORE

*   *   *   *

In 1956 I was invited to become a member, in the place of my grandfather, of the regional committee of the National Trust. I asked Lord Antrim, the chairman, what books I should read on Irish architecture in order to inform myself for the job. He answered that there were none: incredible as it may seem, he was substantially correct. It occurred to me then that, if there were no books on the subject to be read, there must at least be some to be written. I started using my eyes and looking properly at the buildings by which I was surrounded, and found them unexpectedly rewarding. In 1957 I started assembling material for a book on the buildings of Belfast, ultimately published ten years later. I had already a pretty intimate knowledge of the streets of the city through my activity as a Labour Party canvasser; and, by way of the various title-deeds that from time to time passed through my hands, I had more information about the history and development of the town than was available to most people. For two years I spent the greater part of each day's lunch-hour perambulating the streets and alleys of the city centre, looking closely at every single building, and recording my comments in a series of notebooks. These comments were often inane, for it was only in the process of writing that I taught myself the grammar and even the vocabulary of architecture (I still have lapses that scandalise the trained architectural historian). In the process, I came to have a warm and appreciative affection for the odd concatenations of buildings that gave Belfast its very individual character. They ranged from the seemly late-Georgian terraces of College Square, the University district, and Great George's Street, through the crowded but often gaily painted streets of parlour and kitchen houses, to the imposing extravagance of banks, merchant palaces, churches (classical, Italianate, Venetian, or Gothic Revival), and pubs. If ever a book was a labour of love, this was it: and if, as one reviewer remarked, some of my swans were geese, I have no regrets for that.

For, as it turned out, it was published only in the nick of time. A year after it appeared, the Troubles began; and soon after, the bombing campaign. Like other cities, Belfast was already suffering from the double destructive mania of roads engineers and property speculators. Today it is a conservationist's nightmare. There are still a few fine buildings undamaged, but for the most part they are shabby and neglected. Great swathes of desolation sweep through the city, where the planners and traffic engineers have laid out new and over-ambitious

68

road-lines; but ten years later, the roads have still to be built. Gaunt and ugly office blocks, many of them standing unoccupied, have replaced fine stone Victorian warehouses. Steel barrels filled with concrete – mostly rusting – shatter-proof films of plastic glued to window-panes, concrete-block and wire-netting entanglements outside likely targets, and high iron security gates and fences, with metallic exit-only turn-stiles, disfigure the streets of the city centre. Hardly a late-Georgian terrace still stands complete: almost every one is punctuated by gaps where bombed buildings have been demolished. The carcases of bombed-out shops and office blocks stand for years while the com-pensation authorities haggle and niggle with the owners. Churches have lost their stained glass, pubs have lost their etched glass, the windows of both are too often impartially boarded up. In street after street, the majority of the red-brick Victorian or Edwardian terrace houses have been closed, doors and windows crudely filled with con-crete blocks. Thank goodness, there have been no more high-rise blocks of flats, or gallery-access blocks of maisonettes, since the Hous-ing Executive took over from Belfast Corporation and the old Housing Trust; I have had some hand in trying to work out a new and acceptable vernacular for urban redevelopment. Another decade must pass before it is clear whether we have had some success, or whether our mistakes (and mistakes there must be) will prove as egregious as those of our predecessors. In the meanwhile, the demolition men rival the bombers in coarse heartlessness; fine stone-carvings, columnar door-cases, hand-some mantel-pieces, ornate keystones, elegant staircases and balusters, even such simple materials as dressed ashlar and graded slates, all are swept away by bomb or steel ball, by fire or bulldozer, in lorry-loads of smoking rubble: all end up as filling in the Harbour Commissioners' reclamation of the muddy foreshores of Belfast Lough to create new industrial estates.

Since 1956 I have been a committed and devoted conservationist. My interest has been in the artifacts of man, the modest but delightful buildings with which previous generations have endowed the towns, villages, and countryside of Ireland, rather than with the countryside itself or with its wild life. I have devoted more hours than I care to think of to recording, praising, and caring about such buildings – whose merit has been far too little appreciated both by the Irish, and by the rest of the world. But I have watched, in two short decades, while half the heritage of Ulster has been lost. Was ever conservationist more unfortunate in the time and place of his birth?

Yet I have not yet, quite, despaired. There has been a welcome and belated swing in public opinion, across all party and religious divisions, within the past ten years. The bureaucrats, the engineers, the developers, even the councillors, are beginning to respond — here and there. Curiously enough, a shared concern to keep what little is left of a shared heritage may yet serve to bring together aggressively loyalist Ulstermen and aggressively nationalist Irishmen. Is it too much to hope that even the paramilitaries, the gunmen who are the spiritual heirs of those who destroyed the Four Courts, and with them a great part of the history of Ireland, will yet learn to stay their hand? Probably it is; in the past, the destructive element in the Irish character has too often outweighed the constructive element. There are said to be some 10,000 medieval parish churches in England still roofed and used for worship. The corresponding number in Ireland is said to be less than ten. But I am not utterly without hope: and it remains true, as it has been for centuries, that the less there is to save, the more important remains its saving.

TEN

My great-great-grandfather, Wills Hill Brett, born in the 'year of Liberty', received his education at the Belfast Academy under the formidable Dr Bruce. In 1813 he sat his matriculation at Trinity College, Dublin, with ninety-five other candidates; the *Belfast News Letter* reported ten days later – 'Brett, although not yet 16 years old, passed through the entire examination without missing a single word, and got the fifth place, with a certificate of "Valde bene in omnibus". The candidates were examined in Homer, Lucian, Greek Testament, Virgil, Horace, Terence and Sallust'.

He did well at Trinity, though perhaps somewhat harrassed by the letters of his proud and anxious father. In 1814 he sat for a prize but did not get it; his father wrote: 'Well, then, my dearest Wills, to say I wd. not have been gratified and proud of your having got a praemium wd. not be to speak the truth: but I do assure you I am neither hurt nor much disappointed at your not obtaining one'. And in January 1815, after some reproaches regarding his management of his allowance, 'let me again repeat what I have said a hundred times before you entered College: study mankind as well as Greek and Latin books, nor let the study of these latter make you neglect your Writing and Accounts'. It was later in this year that Wills's mother died; it was at this time also that it became clear that Wills was to embrace a career in the Church; his father's letters accordingly became more pious in tone. They had already been quite sufficiently devotional for anyone but an incipient clergyman; that written on the occasion of Wills's confirmation and first communion draws considerably upon the sermons of Jasper Brett, 'an ancestor of your own, a Doctor of Divinity in the Church of Ireland'. It contains some advice of a low-Church, but mildly anti-nonconformist, character: 'during the celebration in church, don't use prayers or ejaculations of your own: they oftener tend to distract the mind (especially of a young person) than anything else: attend devoutly to the clergyman and the delightful service of our church: give your little alms with a cheerful heart: and when the service is ended, retire from church with decent composure, to your own chamber: and *there,* offer up your thanks for the great benefit you have received'.

Wills took his B.A. in 1817; in 1821 he was ordained deacon, and in 1822 priest, when he became incumbent of the parish of Greyabbey, County Down. He was to remain there for twenty-one years, until his translation to Kircubbin in 1843.

These two villages, some five miles apart, lie both on the western shore of the Ards peninsula, looking across Strangford Lough to the distant silhouettes of the Mourne Mountains. It was here that I spent much of my boyhood, at Andrew Bailie's farm at neighbouring Blackabbey. It was near here that Jerome Brett allowed his prisoner to escape from the tower-house of Ardkeen in 1574. Greyabbey was the territory of the Montgomeries of the Ards, and it was here that Bernard Brett had come to find his wife Katherine before 1700. Kircubbin was the property of the Wards of Castleward, and it was amongst them that William Brett had come to find his wife, Thomasene, before 1665.

The incumbency of Greyabbey was by no means an enviable appointment. There was no parsonage, no glebe-house, no glebe; there were no tithes; the total income of the parish was a mere £55 per annum, of which £30 was contributed by composition in lieu of tithes by the three lay improprietors, Lord Londonderry, Mr Montgomery, and Mr Auchinleck. Wills Brett seems to have taken lodgings in the village and to have spent his weekends there, but until his father's death; most of his time was still spent at Charleville. In 1824 he officiated at the wedding of his elder sister Matilda to a young linen merchant, John Willson, in Newtownbreda church. In the following year he took part in an even more solemn ceremony: the funeral of the 'young and reverend' Edward Montgomery of Portaferry. The burial took place between nine and ten o'clock of a summer evening in the family vault in the imposing ruins of Greyabbey:

The interment of the Rev. E. Montgomery was really an affecting scene. The sorrow apparent on the countenances of the assembled multitude, the downcast looks of his affectionate relatives, the solemn and impressive manner in which the Rev. Mr. Brett read the funeral service, the serenity of the evening, the fainter glimmerings of waxen candles substituted for the departing light of an almost vertical sun, the surrounding monuments of the ancient Montgomery family; and the whole encompassed by the ruined walls of a once magnificent Abbey, in the midst of a hall in which the voice of revelry once rose high, but in which the only sounds now heard are 'the moaning of the wind, and the melancholy croaking of the raven' – all this was surely calculated to elevate the affections far beyond the transitory enjoyments of this world, to raise the mind from nature to nature's GOD.

As a sometime journalist, I can well appreciate how the writer in the *Belfast News Letter* got carried away, even to the extent of misplacing revelry in the nave of a twelfth-century abbey. So far as I have been able to find, this was the only occasion when Wills Brett's performance was reported in the press: despite a promising start, he was not to achieve fame as a preacher. Indeed, I know very little of his early years in the Church. There survive a few scraps of notes for sermons, in some cases with shopping lists or personal *aides-memoire* scribbled on the back: 'Mutton for W.T., do. for self; wind clocks; visit 3 sick poor; see Mr. Taylor'.

There is also a strange and passionate prayer, meticulously initialled and dated 'Charleville, Thursday night 1st February 1827':

O Almighty Lord, everlasting GOD! Maker of Heaven and Earth, Judge of All men! a vile worm, yea, a most miserable, unworthy sinner falls at the footstool of thy grace, who hath nothing to plead in his behalf –

.   .   .   .

From my mother's womb until this very hour I have been adding sin to sin – I was born in sin, & am the child of wrath. I am unworthy of the least of thy mercies, & deserve nothing but everlasting destruction from the presence of the Lord & from the glory of his power.

Yet I cleave to thee, O my Lord, as my only hope: O remember not the sins & offences of my youth: O cast me not away from thy presence: O take not thy holy spirit from me – above all, O my gracious GOD!, leave me not to myself & the plague of my own heart, for I am very abominable, I am, in a word, *a sink of sin* – O my GOD, I confess to thee, & to thee alone, that my flesh lusteth against thy Holy Spirit: O cleanse & purify it as thine own temple –

.   .   .   .

If it be thy good pleasure, guide me by thy secret, but sure, providence to a partner in life, who is *a Christian indeed* – that she may be such a help-mate as becometh a minister of thy Word. If this my request be not granted, make me, I beseech thee, perfectly contented: but keep me single, or save my partner & myself, so that, what thou joinest in this life, may not be separated in the next.

Celibacy must have lain heavy on the young man of twenty-nine; I should have hesitated to reproduce so very personal and intimate a prayer – 'I confess to thee & to thee alone' – but for the fact that it was neatly written out, and most carefully folded and preserved amongst Wills Brett's few surviving papers; from which I conclude that he did not intend to deprive posterity of it. In the event, he had to wait another seven years before his prayer was answered, and he was provided with a help-mate.

In the meanwhile, he set off, soon after his father's death, upon a kind of ecclesiastical tour of the industrial midlands of England. Wills Brett belonged to the evangelical or low-Church wing even of the Church of Ireland, always much 'lower' in tone than the Church of England. He left a lengthy memorandum, dated June 1830, from The Hough, Stafford, giving an account of a Church Missionary Society meeting at Newcastle-under-Lyme; how he preached to a meeting of 700 persons at Wrexham, but the collection was only £18, compared to £28 at the much smaller meeting the previous night; how he preached again in the parish church of Newcastle to a good congregation, including '150 Highlanders present on their march through – much attention – afternoon – I preached at the new church – too large and noisy'. 'I hope the trip was of some service to the cause and to myself, but felt the effects of it afterwards in weakness, lowness, & want of vigor – so that I *now* see that these excitements are to be used with great caution'.

I cannot help but see a good deal of resemblance between my great-great-grandfather and the Rev. Theobald Pontifex in Samuel Butler's *Way of All Flesh*. They were, indeed, near-contemporaries: Wills was born in 1798, Theobald in 1802; Theobald married his Christina in 1831, Wills his Mattie in 1835; though Theobald lived till 1881, Wills only till 1862.

Wills Brett's wife was Mattie (baptised Martha) Garrett, daughter of a Belfast solicitor. Aged twenty-six when she married, she was a woman of literary and musical tastes. She was interested in botany, and contributed to Sir Joseph Hooker's *British Flora*. Family tradition has it that she spent most of her life, when not bearing children, lying on a sofa studying Greek and Hebrew texts. It was fortunate that Wills Brett inherited private means from his father, and that household duties could safely be left to the servants and 'Nursey'. The family was a very musical one. Wills 'had a beautiful voice, and sang very well, and did a great deal in a remote country parish to improve church music. He sang the leading airs in the Messiah beautifully'. Mattie 'was a pupil of the great Bunting' (a frequent visitor to Charleville), and 'had herself an exquisite touch on the piano. She had one maxim – "Good music, or none" '. Charleville was sold a month after the wedding, and the young couple moved to a rented house at Greyabbey. Thirteen children were born, at regular intervals, of whom ten survived, and three died in infancy. By the time the youngest was born, Wills Brett was fifty-six, Mattie forty-five.

Private means or no – and his were by no means limitless – it was plainly unsatisfactory to try to bring up so large a family in a parish with only a tiny stipend, and no parsonage. The Church of Ireland was undergoing a drastic reorganisation at the hands of Parliament as a result of the tithes war of the 1830s. Since most of the tithes of Grey-abbey had been commuted, this did not much affect Wills Brett, but hundreds of his fellow-clergy were at this period 'reduced almost to destitution'. The next-door parish to Greyabbey was the Union of Ballywalter, comprising three formerly separate parishes. The Commissioners of Ecclesiastical Inquiry noted in 1831 – 'It is observed that after different fruitless efforts to reside, the incumbent has been compelled, by the repeated illnesses of his wife, to give up permanent residence in the parish'; so the whole large area was entrusted by him to a curate. This state of affairs was regarded as unsatisfactory both by the Commissioners and by Mr Robert Ward of Bangor, the local landowner. The former resolved to divide the united parishes so soon as the present incumbent should retire or die; but Mr Ward resolved to endow the village of Kircubbin with church, parsonage, and parson without waiting. And so, in 1843, Mr Ward built a new classical church in an unexpected Greek-revival style, rare in Ulster, in the main street; a large and commodious new parsonage on the hill behind the village; endowed both with a sum of 3½ per cent, stock, which brought in £140 a year; and, after some rather complicated negotiations with the Bishop, presented his protégé Wills Brett to the living.

This arrangement had its oddities: the new church was never properly constituted a separate parish. Wills Brett received some incredulous letters from his friend the Rev. Hull, formerly a curate in nearby Innishargy, now episcopal minister in a parish in the highlands of Scotland: 'Is it so, that henceforth there are to be no fewer than 4 ministers of the Establishment including yourself? . . .If they be all spiritual men, you will doubtless receive much mutual refreshment and comfort from Christian intercourse; an advantage I vary rarely indeed enjoy. . . . Scottish episcopacy is leprous with popery. Evangelical clergymen are quite black sheep here'. Mr Hull's letters bring a breath from the outer world into the country parsonage. In 1847, the opening year of the Great Famine, he comments on the outbreak of fever in Kircubbin, and on the 'works of mercy' being organised by Wills Brett. He also recommends to Mattie, who has been ill, a new miracle drug: 'I would here beg to commend, in the strongest manner, a new medicine, which is of special efficiency in strengthening the human constitution: it is Cod Liver Oil'.

The Famine years were less catastrophic in County Down than in the south and west of Ireland, but conditions were bad nonetheless, especially in the Ards peninsula; anyone who knows that countryside will know how many ruins of roofless and abandoned cottages are still to be found there. There are several references to the Famine in letters to Wills Brett from his aunt Elizabeth Corne: 'If you had seen the number of miserable looking creatures that went down this avenue yesterday, your heart would have been grieved — not less than 700 who were going to Crossgar for tickets to work on the road — their wages a shilling a day'. And: 'You are all going to do a noble act by setting up a Public Bakery and all the other helps you are getting for the poor'.

Wills, when either he or his wife was away from home, was a tireless correspondent, writing to Mattie almost daily — sometimes twice in one day. His slanting handwriting is atrocious, sometimes quite indecipherable; he was much given to the use of abbreviations — Greyabbey is 'G.A.' and Kircubbin 'K.C.'. The education of the boys was a constant concern. Charles, the eldest, was never sent to school at all, but was taught at home by his parents. His father intended him for the Church, but to this young Charles demurred: he went so far as to tell his father that he could not accept the Thirty-Nine Articles, upon which he was sent to Belfast at the age of thirteen and articled to his uncle Thomas Garrett as a solicitor. Wills Brett was very angry about this, and relations between father and son were never completely restored. However, questions as to his lodgings, board, and laundry gave rise to constant concern. Thomas, the second son, was sent to boarding school at Portora, Co. Fermanagh, and thence to Trinity College, Dublin; in 1858 Wills Brett accompanied him there to sit his entrance exam, and both took the opportunity of hearing as much music as they could. Thomas later became a well-known but eccentric practitioner at the Bar in London. In 1858 George was sent to share Charles's lodgings in Belfast, where he was apprenticed to a firm of export brokers. He was to end up as an accountant in New Zealand. Both the youngest boys entered the law: Robert became a barrister and practised on the Kerry circuit: Jasper established himself as a solicitor in Dublin.

Wills Brett died, aged sixty-four, in June 1862. He left an estate of between £4,000 and £5,000, divided amongst his children in such a way that the youngest ones (who would need it most) received the most, the eldest least. Charles, who acted as executor, received only a legacy of £20, perhaps because of the Thirty-Nine Articles. All the legacy and succession-duty papers were neatly completed and tidily filed away in the family office by young Charles Brett. The assets included a cow valued at £12 15s.; a heifer valued at £6 17s. 6d.; and a piano valued at £3 5s. The family had to leave the parsonage, of course; they rented a newly built house at Carlisle Circus, Belfast, where Mattie and eight of her children took up residence, with Charles, then aged twenty-four, as the breadwinner of the family. Later, when Charles got married, mother and daughters moved to a house in the Crescent, Holywood. There Mattie died aged seventy-five in 1886. In 1881 the youngest of the girls married one George MacKisack, and emigrated with him to New Zealand. It rather looks as though he left his country for his country's good; my great-grandfather lent him large sums of money; he died in 1892, leaving seven small children, and a fulsome obituary in the *Otago Daily Times* – 'He was a faithful servant to his employers, over whose premises the flag was displayed half-mast high out of respect to his memory, and he was highly respected amongst business men and among his private acquaintances'. Beside this, great-grandfather has written 'A lie!' and below 'He was an infernal scoundrel. C.H.B. Oct 92'.

The other girls never married, and lived together for the rest of their lives in Holywood – Elizabeth Corne died in 1893, Annabella Matilda in 1928, Anne Catherine in 1929, and Mary in 1935. I remember being taken to see my great-great-aunt Mary when I was about six. She was a little old lady in a lace cap sitting up in bed. I have a much more vivid recollection of the enormous fluffy grey cat, which towered above me as it stood on the bed. It was called Phyllis Doreen, I am told, and was a tom-cat. I remember too being taken to the house in the Crescent after Aunt Mary's death, and being told I might choose one book as a memento from a large number laid out on the floor. I chose Peter

Parley's *Tales about Animals*. It was a good choice: it is full of curious anecdotes and delightful woodcuts, some of them from originals by Thomas Bewick. It is inscribed on the flyleaf, 'Presented to the Juvenile Brettish Association of Kircubbin by J.R.G., 30th March 1848'. J.R.G. was my great-great-great-uncle James Ramsay Garrett, then a partner in the firm in which I am a partner now.

ELEVEN

I would be regarded by most Ulster people (to whom religious affiliation is of absorbing interest) as coming of a strongly Church of Ireland
family. Though Wills Hill Brett was the only clergyman amongst my
direct ancestors, his father had been a layman of edifying piety; Jasper
Brett, Dr John Brett, and William Brett had all been clergymen in the
eighteenth century; to come nearer home, my grandfather and my
father were both active and diligent laymen – and since disestablishment, the laity have played a far larger part in the affairs of the
Church of Ireland than they do in the sister Church of England.

Over the years, I have gradually become detached from the Church
of my forebears. Not long indeed after being confirmed at the age of
thirteen, I began to question the beliefs in which I had been brought up.
For some years, I devoted many anxious hours of thought, and many
reams of paper, to the question of what I believed: I read a good deal of
simple theology, philosophy, and metaphysics without feeling much
the wiser. By the time I had arrived at Oxford, I had settled into a kind
of defensive neutrality: I described myself as an agnostic, but I was
quite willing to attend the services of any denomination or religion. I
did, in fact, enjoy good church music, and good church architecture,
and the vestments, chants, and incense of Roman Catholic and Greek
Orthodox worship: but I was clear enough in my mind that it was the
aesthetics, not the beliefs, that gave me satisfaction. I am afraid my
low-Church great-great-grandfather would have been sadly shocked.

Since then my views have hardened. The more I have seen of the
different brands of Christianity at work in Ulster, the more I have
come to dislike them; and especially the clergy (which is not to say that
there are not some clergymen, of all denominations, whom I admire
and respect as individuals). It is astonishing how often an Ulsterman
gets asked, especially by outsiders, the direct question: 'Are you a
Protestant or a Catholic?' To this, if I do not wish to give undue
offence, I reply: 'I am an interdenominational anti-clerical'. If, on the
other hand, the question is posed (as it often is) in a way that is impertinent (and the most recent person to ask me it in this way was Lord
Longford), I answer, 'I am a militant atheist'. This, though not strictly

quite true, often produces agreeably startled reactions: Lord Longford's was more rewarding than most: 'Then it is you', he cried, 'who ought to be interned in Long Kesh'. As to atheism, I find myself unable to believe in the kind of God postulated by any of the Churches, or for that matter by Mohammedans, Jews, or Buddhists. But I cannot deny that there are aspects of human existence that are inaccessible to human reason; if 'God' means those elements and forces in life that are incomprehensible, then I can believe in its existence with perfect cheerfulness. Lest, on the strength of these innocent confidences, someone may try to recruit me into the humanist camp, I must point out hastily that humanists hold jumble-sales and other such-like corporate acts of worship, and are therefore as bad as the rest. For it is organised religion to which I object: and above all, the kind of organised religion that demands and imposes the belief that it, and it alone, is right.

If all the Christians of Northern Ireland were to be expatriated and resettled in the Falkland Islands, and if the British Government were then gracefully to concede the claims of Argentina, life would be very much pleasanter and more peaceable for those few Ulstermen who were left.

But I must ruefully admit, for all the intemperate secularism of that Swiftian proposal, that I remain to some extent the prisoner of my upbringing. I find something unsatisfying in the Roman Catholic form of service, especially now that the Mass is said in English. I find the Presbyterian tradition of extempore prayer profoundly off-putting. I find myself not altogether out of sympathy with Charles Brett of Charleville, when he wrote to his son Wills at Trinity of 'the delightful service of our church': I like the stately roll of seventeenth-century English: I like the seemly stylisation of its forms and ceremonies. I have, sadly, had occasion to go to the funerals of many friends, Catholic, Presbyterian, and Church of Ireland. I never leave the church on such an occasion without thinking to myself, *malgré moi* – 'Perhaps I am an atheist, but if I am, I am a Church of Ireland atheist'.

*   *   *   *

Nothing more disconcerted me, when I came home to live in Ulster, than the intolerance of my Protestant colleagues. Though I have had to learn to live with it, it disconcerts me still. And, most puzzling and disconcerting of all, those who hold the most bigoted and intolerant opinions are sometimes, when seen as individuals, the nicest and most estimable people.

I have had something more than a nodding acquaintance with Dr Ian Paisley for over twenty years. In the early fifties, when he was first shaping his own Free Presbyterian Church and his individual form of extreme-Protestant politics, we patronised the same inexpensive printer: I, in the interests of the Labour Party; he, in connection with a campaign to oust a more-moderate-than-usual Unionist M.P., the late Brian Maginness, from the Iveagh constituency of County Down. It was soon after this, in 1956, that Dr Paisley was alleged to have played a part in the 'abduction' of a young Catholic girl, Maura Lyons, from her family, so that she might be brought up in the true Protestant faith. Dr Paisley has denied the allegation. A few years later, he flaunted around Stormont an enormous red ensign and a placard, 'No Mass, No Lemass'. I abhorred it when he spoke contemptuously of the Pope as 'old red-socks'. Taking it by and large, I have abhorred almost everything Dr Paisley has ever said in the pulpit, on the election platform, or in Parliament. His words and actions during the unsuccessful U.W.A.C. strike were, it seems to me, utterly indefensible, and very possibly led to loss of life. Yet, in private conversation, I have never found Dr Paisley unreasonable or discourteous; and I know of at least one occasion when he acted with great generosity and humanity towards a young Catholic political opponent. What is one to make of inconsistencies such as this? Though I detest all Dr Paisley stands for in public, and rather like him in private, I do not think he is a hypocrite. He is a basically decent man who has been led astray by the intensity of his own prejudices; and I should say exactly the same of some of his Catholic opposite numbers.

Before I went to boarding school, my parents used to take me to see the Orange processions in Belfast on the twelfth of July. These are really very extraordinary occasions. Thousands upon thousands of Ulster Protestants parade in their best suits, wearing bowler hats, sashes or collarettes, and curious cuff adornments; carrying deacon-poles, halberds, swords, and flags; each lodge headed by its banner, a great square of silk with bunches of orange lilies tied to its poles, portraying some suitable scene from Orange mythology – King Billy crossing the Boyne, or Queen Victoria presenting the Bible to the Heathen, or the Earl of Beaconsfield, or a recently deceased Worshipful Master. Each lodge is preceded by a band, hired for the day: sometimes pipes, sometimes flutes, sometimes silver or brass, sometimes squeeze-boxes or accordeons; all playing hymns or party tunes. Nothing could be more piquant than the contrast between the gymnastic antics of drum-majors, drum-majorettes, and juvenile imitators, twirling and hurling their ornate staffs into the air, and the grimly devoted expressions on the faces of the Brethren themselves. The night before the Twelfth is the Eleventh Night; when bonfires are lit in all the Protestant streets of Ulster: there is revelry, there is drunkenness, there is dancing in the streets; the little boys enjoy themselves beyond anything that would seem possible. This religious festival celebrates the revenge of Orange King William in 1690 for the indignities imposed by the Catholics in 1641 and 1688. Yet, if one could ignore the political and sectarian symbolism, it is very like the Catholic fiestas of the Mediterranean world; the saints' days of southern Italy, Sicily, and Malta; the gypsy festival of the Saintes-Maries-de-la-Mer.

I well remember taking part in those festivities in the late 'fifties, when groups of us – Catholic, Protestant, and neither – could make our way from end to end of the Sandy Row or the Shankill Road, joining in the dancing or the bonfire parties as we went, taking a bottle of stout first in this pub, then in that. James Boyce was usually leader of the party; no questions were asked; a Catholic was as welcome as a Prod; it really seemed that, at long last, the Orange celebrations had cast off their anti-Catholic associations, and were developing into a folk celebration of a harmless and delightful kind. At the time, I thought that the march of progress would overtake the Orange march; that the modern world of radio, and television, and democracy (for which a war had lately been fought and won) would prevail over the old loyalties and superstitions; that the Orangemen would go the way of the Free Foresters and the Morris dancers. But I was wrong.

The Orange Order provides a colourful symbol of Ulster Protestantism. My great-grandfather came to hate it. In his youth, it had seemed a sort of populist movement with liberal and reforming tendencies, and so he was prepared to countenance the electoral alliance between Thomas McClure, the Liberal candidate for whom he acted as agent in 1868, and the Orange leader, Johnston of Ballykilbeg. As the years passed, he changed his mind; in successive Home Rule riots, in the troubled times before and after the Great War, he saw militant Orangeism spring to the aid of militant Protestantism – and not always in a defensive posture. My own opinions have followed much the same course. In peaceful times, the Orange Order has many virtues; it acts as a sort of friendly society for its members; it brings participation in vivid forms of folk-art within the reach of ordinary working men; the lodge provides a social life, the Orange Hall (especially in the country) a community centre. But in times of tension, it becomes a secret society, not merely as its members claim, a society with secrets; it acts as a focus for bigotry and extremism; it invites onto its platforms, and to the pulpits at its religious services, only those Protestant clergy who can be trusted to be outspoken in their hostility to Rome. The connection between Orangeism and the Protestant paramilitary armies of the present day is unproven; it is probably untrue that a majority of Orangemen are paramilitaries; but I suspect it to be true that a majority of Protestant paramilitaries are Orangemen.

Having said which, I am back full circle: some of the most decent and honourable men I know are Orangemen.

*   *   *   *

There was a significant relaxation of sectarian tensions in the late 'fifties and early 'sixties, especially amongst the urban working classes. In part this was due to the refusal of the Catholic community at large to support the I.R.A. campaign of violence of the years between 1956 and 1962; a campaign that, at the time, looked vicious enough, though with the hindsight of the 1970s it was a feeble gesture. It had not been possible before, and it was not to be possible later, for Catholics to mingle unchallenged in the Protestant crowds that celebrated the Eleventh Night and the Twelfth Day.

In 1963 the ageing Lord Brookeborough retired from the premiership of Northern Ireland. A man of great suavity, wit, and personal charm, he was nonetheless a Unionist of the old school, and made no bones about it: one of the last survivors of the days of the Ulster Covenant, Lord Carson, and James Craig. He wore his Orange cuffs and collarette as comfortably as he wore his tweeds; whereas his successor, Terence O'Neill, looked thoroughly uncomfortable and self-conscious when photographed in his regalia. The old generation was passing away from politics in Dublin, too – it began to look as though Ireland, both north and south, was prepared to put the past behind it, and inch its way into the modern world. O'Neill began to make very tentative advances towards the Catholic minority within the state; he did not move far or fast; but these new developments struck alarm into the breasts of the custodians of traditional Protestantism. A body called Ulster Protestant Action became increasingly vocal, and began to pick up increasing support. Posters began to appear on the walls of Protestant districts that made outsiders begin to feel, once again, that they were unwelcome. The Orange backlash had already begun to gather its strength.

*   *   *   *

The extreme Protestant point of view is very simple, and it is very logical. We are in a large majority, it states with perfect truth, in our own province; this is a democracy, and in a democracy it must be accepted that the will of the majority must prevail; therefore we are entitled as of right to impose our own standards and beliefs on a minority that does not share them. But the over-simple logic breaks down in the face of reality. In the first place, the unit of democracy in Ulster comprises not a single community, but two communities with differing aspirations and traditions – the majority in Ulster is the minority in Ireland as a whole. In the second place, there has never been a semblance of an alternation between parties; the Protestants have been permanent top dogs, the Catholics permanent under-dogs. In the third place, the majority has too often (not always, certainly, but too often) abused its position, and acted over-bearingly, with a mixture of arrogance and insensitivity, towards a minority with no means of release but emigration: which is, of course, an unpalatable kind of surrender.

Over the years, this arrogance has taken many forms: both in big things, and in small things. The biggest was the refusal, until it was too late, to concede the principle of 'one man, one vote'. The shortcomings from this principle were comparatively trivial: Catholics as such were not deprived of voting rights: reform, in line with post-war British practice, could not conceivably change the balance of Ulster politics: the worst it could do (as it did) was to give the Catholic citizens of Derry a majority on their own local council. The most trivial, but by no means the least mischievous, was the determination of Protestants to impose their own convention of sabbath-keeping on a community with a quite different tradition of treating Sunday as a day for legitimate recreation. This 300-Year War – for it has been going on in Ulster without interruption since the Puritan days of the seventeenth century — has not been fought to a standstill yet; the Sunday closing of municipal swimming-pools, golf courses, leisure centres, and playing fields is as live an issue as it has ever been. One battle in this long-fought war I witnessed at close quarters; its consequences were to be a good deal more far-ranging than any of its participants realised at the time.

In 1958 the Northern Ireland Labour Party made a political breakthrough: after years without any representation in the Stormont parliament, four of its candidates won seats, though only by the slimmest of majorities. In 1962 the same four were returned with much increased majorities, and though none of the other Labour candidates was elected, the total Unionist vote in the sixteen Belfast constituencies was only 8,000 ahead of the Labour Party's 62,000. At long last, it seemed, both Protestant and Catholic voters were preparing to abandon the old loyalties and vote for a non-sectarian opposition party. Labour was beginning to recruit young Catholic members in increasing numbers; the time had come to start fighting for representation in the Republican and Nationalist strongholds. In April 1963, as outgoing chairman of the party, I made a speech emphasising that point:

> In the past ten years, Labour has fought elections in Protestant seats with Protestant candidates, but its beliefs and reputation for integrity have earned us much Catholic support. The first and paramount battle has been with the Unionists, the party in power representing what I might perhaps call the Protestant vested interests. I believe that the time has come when we must challenge the Catholic vested interests as well as the Protestant ones.

This shift of policy was well received amongst the younger generation of Catholics, seeking a constructive outlet for their energies, and in fact two of the six Labour councillors elected to the City Hall in May 1964 were Catholics. But it was not welcomed by the diehard Protestant element, which still existed even within the Labour Party. The public image of the party still depended on its four M.P.s at Stormont, on the attitudes they adopted and the opinions they expressed. All four were, as it happened, Protestants of notable piety, though of varied kinds. Tom Boyd, leader of the party, Presbyterian patternmaker, was the most relaxed and easy-going; he had no objection to sipping a glass of cider in a pub, whereas his three colleagues were teetotallers of the most rigid kind. Vivian Simpson, former Methodist missionary, then shop-keeper, had been born in Dublin and worked in Africa, and was generally tolerant in his outlook, though a man very deeply committed to his religion. David Bleakley, school-teacher and Church of Ireland lay reader, had started in the shipyard, obtained a trade-union scholarship to Ruskin College, Oxford, and taken a degree at Queen's University; a fiery and effective orator, he retained despite his education something of the narrowness of his early upbringing. Billy Boyd, shipyard worker and Methodist lay preacher, had come into the Labour Party through youth work in the boys' clubs of the Shankill Road: he too retained a very strong identification with the Protestantism of his working-class background. As it happened, and it was to be significant, David Bleakley and Billy Boyd sat for mainly Protestant constituencies: Tom Boyd and Vivian Simpson for mixed constituencies.

For many years, all the children's playgrounds in Belfast had been closed, and the swings and slides chained, on Sundays, at the insistence of the dominant Protestant majority; a petty restriction, which was viewed by Catholic parents, especially in mixed areas of the city, with vast irritation. Early in 1964, as part of its programme for the municipal elections, the Labour Party had stated unambiguously: 'Labour will support the opening of children's playgrounds and recreational facilities on Sunday for those who wish to use them'. On the strength of this document, six candidates had been elected. But when, in November 1964, a resolution to open the playgrounds came before the Corporation, three of the Protestant Labour councillors, led by Billy Boyd, voted against or abstained; and in consequence the motion was lost by one vote. For his part, Boyd, who was certainly subject to much extreme-Protestant pressure within his constituency, declined to treat the question as one either of conscience or of politics, but somewhat disingenuously if not unreasonably explained that 'he had no particular views on Sunday observance, but he opposed play-centres being opened because elderly residents in nearby houses feared their opening would bring in undesirable elements'. The reaction of the recent Catholic recruits was indignant: two, including one of the recently elected councillors, resigned from the party. The Irish newspapers took the matter up, accusing the Labour Party of narrow-minded Sabbatarianism. Amused and intrigued, the English press took the matter up too. The party membership was deeply divided; most branches demanded disciplinary action, a few from Protestant areas supported Boyd. This public split was bad enough: it was made far worse, however, when David Bleakley supported Boyd, and the affair took on the aspect (so far as the public was concerned) of a struggle between the policy-making bodies of the party and its Protestant representatives in Stormont and at the City Hall.

The 'Sunday Swings' affair, as it was called, led to weeks of special meetings, deputations, disciplinary resolutions, negotiations, and attempts at compromise; I was in the thick of them all. Tempers ran high, expulsions and resignations flew about in all directions, personal animosities came to the surface; matters were not helped by Billy Boyd's mulish truculence, by David Bleakley's stinging eloquence, nor by my own intransigence. At that time, in the heat of the moment, I said (and wrote) things that I should perhaps today rephrase more moderately. But the question of principle refused to go away. Billy Boyd was, in fact, expelled from the Labour Party, but David Bleakley used his vote to prevent the decision from being given effect by the equally divided Stormont Parliamentary Party. In the end, a compromise was patched up, some watery undertakings were given and accepted, and Boyd was allowed back into the fold. To my high indignation, a meaningless statement was issued to the press: for the benefit of my colleagues, I appended a sarcastic foot-note to its concluding paragraph: 'This means that, due to outside pressures, the Executive Committee is afraid to carry out its duty to give a ruling on the interpretation of an entirely unambiguous sentence in the Party's policy statement, and has accordingly agreed that the whole matter should be hushed up until the public has forgotten about it'.

But the public did not forget about it: the party had lost credit both with Catholic and Protestant voters: the trend towards the acceptance of Labour as a non-sectarian alternative was reversed, and at the following general election, in November 1965, the party suffered a crushing defeat; not only did it fail to win more of the seats that had been so nearly in its grasp at the previous election, it actually lost two of those it held.

I have not recounted this old and sorry story in such detail because I want to rake over old sores, or because I want to apportion blame — I am sure I bear as much of the blame as anyone else. I have told it because it illustrates how large a part the symbolism of intrinsically small matters plays in the constant conflict between Protestant and Catholic traditions and ways of life. And because it still seems to me a most melancholy example of the way in which the Protestant community and its representatives so often refuse to act with understanding and generosity in those small matters where concessions could bring richly disproportionate rewards.

*   *   *   *

Another example of the Protestant determination to force its will on everyone else in Ulster was the Ulster Workers' Council strike of 1974. The overwhelming effectiveness of this, the first general strike in the British Isles since 1926, depended on the loyalist convictions of a comparatively small number of key workers in the power stations. They had discovered their strength in the purely economic work-to-rule of 1970. This knowledge had been put to use during the two-day strike of 1972, immediately following the dissolution of the Stormont parliament and the introduction of direct rule from London; and again in 1973, after the internment of the first Protestants. Although none of these occasions could be counted a political success for the strikers, they served to show how devastating could be the effects of widespread electricity cuts. The fortnight's strike of May 1974 came very close to causing the total collapse of the community; it did, in fact, succeed in bringing down the six-month-old power-sharing government that had been formed by Brian Faulkner.

The strike started on Wednesday 15 May; that was a day of power cuts, of road blocks and barricades, the disruption of transport, the intimidation of shops and small businesses, and the shut-down of the shipyard and the major factories. As in the previous strikes, a surprising number of office workers managed to find their way into work, trickling by devious routes through or round the obstacles. In my office, as in many others, work continued after a fashion, though it was wise to keep well away from the front windows to avoid attracting the attention of roaming bands of tartan youths. But as the days went by, the amount of work actually done became less and less; and attendance at the office became something of a token. The lack of heating and artificial lighting was no great deprivation in the month of May: but, as the ever longer and more frequent power cuts took effect, so without warning electric typewriters, photocopiers, accounting machines, suddenly became dead and useless. By the end of the first week, power cuts were lasting for twelve hours at a time. The telephone service was already unreliable; postal deliveries were few and unpredictable. On 22

May the strikers imposed a total ban on oil and petrol supplies, so the use of private cars, already perilous with so many barricades and hi-jackers in the streets, came to an almost complete stop. The bakeries and the dairies had closed down; food shops were allowed to open during limited hours, but supplies could not be got to them, stocks were running low, queues outside were interminable. On that Satur-day, the tenth day of the strike, the Prime Minister, Harold Wilson, made his ill-judged television broadcast in which he referred to the Ulster workers as 'spongers': this, predictably, was to swing the sup-port of most uncommitted Ulster Protestants behind the strikers. On the Monday, when the army was at long last ordered to take over petrol deliveries – a decision coming too late to be effective in any event – the U.W.C. announced a final and total stoppage of all essen-tial services: the complete cut-off of electricity, gas, water, sewage, and telephones. The following day, Faulkner resigned; the strikers had won; and on the morning of 29 May the return to work, and to a normal existence, began.

So far as my own office was concerned, the gravest threat was the stoppage of the sewage stations. The centre of Belfast is low-lying, and the basements of our office (which since the bomb of 1972 had been pressed into service as offices) lay below high-tide level. If the pumping station at the end of our street closed down, we might expect twice-daily floods of mixed sewage and sea-water to back up the drains and flood the basement to a depth of four or five feet. My father, full of helpful reminiscences, recollected a day forty years earlier when this had happened, and he had seen the model yacht belonging to the then caretaker's little boy come sailing up the basement stairs. It was imposs-ible to move all the papers and documents from the safes and filing-cabinets. After some thought, I concluded that the best precaution open to us was to seal the openings around their doors and drawers; but what with? All the shops, of course, had long since closed; with some resourcefulness (as I now think) I bicycled round the houses of those friends who had children, commandeering all their plasticine, and forced long multi-coloured cylinders of this disagreeable material into every crack in every safe and every filing-cabinet. In the event, the pumping stations did not stop, and the hardest part of the return to normal when the strike had ended proved to be the removal of the plasticine caulking.

During these last days of the strike, I found it possible to get from my home, some four miles away on the Malone ridge, to the office by using one of my children's bicycles. The journey downhill was notice-ably easier than the return trip; but at least, on a bicycle, it was not too difficult to turn the flanks of the barricades at various points on the route. My father advised me to be very careful; during a similar stop-page of public transport in the troubles of 1912, my grandfather had used the same means of transport, but the front wheel of his bicycle had got stuck in the tramlines at Shaftesbury Square, he had been thrown by his mount, had broken his leg, and spent six weeks in hospital.

If there were difficulties at the office, there were difficulties at home also. My wife and family were all, as it happened, away in England, leaving behind them a pretty adequate stock of food. Just in time, before stocks ran out, we had acquired some paraffin and a camping cooker, which (despite a considerable want of aptitude) I taught myself to use for basic cookery. At all hours of day and night, one listened on a transistor radio to the news bulletins, and heard the ever-more-lugubrious prophecies of Hugo Patterson, the spokesman for the electricity service: 'this shut-down is complete, it's final, it's irrevoc-able' — 'we are past the point of no return'. Though issued, no doubt, in good faith, these statements were untrue and misleading; the power workers were in fact nursing their plant at minimum power with very great skill, in such a way that no irreparable damage was done; Hugo Patterson was their most effective (if involuntary) ally, and probably contributed as much as Harold Wilson to the final success of the strike.

It was a curious experience to sit each evening, in the gathering dusk — no street-lights anywhere, only the faintest of flickering lights in the windows of neighbouring houses — isolated in the midst of a com-munity that had suffered almost total social break-down; wondering what would happen next. The feeling of helplessness was very great: no positive action whatever was possible. Was it a bit like this in the drawing-rooms of St Petersburg in October 1917? My own course of action was simple and logical: I made myself as comfortable as I could, and found that, in the process, I was returning to the simpler life of my eighteenth-century ancestors. I lit a roaring fire in the drawing-room. I found the silver candle-sticks with the falcon crest, and lit the room with candles. I had recently bought a case of claret; each evening, I opened a bottle, and fuddled myself comfortably by fire-light and candle-light. Only the gloomy muttering and nattering of the transistor radio at my side distinguished my May evenings from those that Wil-liam Brett might have spent by his fireside at Ballynewport, Charles Brett at Killough, or his son Charles Brett at Charleville.

TWELVE

Mattie Garrett, who had married Wills Brett in 1835, was the eldest daughter of an attorney born in Belfast in 1774. The family firm of Ramsay & Garrett was certainly in existence by 1806, and was probably founded several years earlier. The original partners were Mattie's father, Thomas, and James Ramsay, both of whom had links with the United Irishmen.

I do not know where or when James Ramsay was born – his papers have not survived. He died in 1822, and was described as 'an eminent solicitor, practising in Belfast for a long series of years'. But he may not have been as old as this would imply. In 1806 Dr Drennan wrote from Dublin to Mrs McTier: 'I imagine a young, active Attorney rather in search of business, than too much occupied, would be the fittest. . . . Do you know of any such in Belfast who is of good character? Is Ramsay?' Unfortunately her reply is not preserved, but Drennan subsequently employed him (though about 1810 he complained 'the Attorney Ramsey is not speedy'). Dr Drennan was very likely influenced in his choice by the fact that, in 1803, Ramsay had offered his services, free of charge, in the defence of Thomas Russell at Downpatrick on a charge of treason.

Russell had been one of the leaders of the United Irishmen, and a member of the idealistic literary coterie of Northern intellectuals who had drawn their inspiration from the French Revolution. In 1794 he was appointed librarian of the Belfast Linenhall Library; in 1796 he rashly signed his own name, and the description 'An United Irishman', to a pamphlet on Catholic emancipation. That summer he was appointed military commander for County Down, and in September was arrested on a charge of high treason and imprisoned in turn at Kilmainham, Newgate, and Fort George in Scotland. He was accordingly out of circulation at the time of the '98 rising; in 1802, after nearly six years of internment without trial, he was set free – the Peace of Amiens had just been signed – and allowed to go to Paris. He returned secretly to Ireland in 1803, and was sent to Ulster, as General-in-Chief of the Northern District, to take command of the last desperate attempt at revolution in that year. But the people of the North this time refused to rise: Russell fled to Dublin, where he was arrested, and returned for trial to Downpatrick.

There he was attended by James Ramsay, bearing letters and money from Mary Ann McCracken. The trial was taken very seriously by the authorities — a troop of cavalry and no less than 600 yeomen mounted guard over the court-house. Russell wrote, 'My intention was to have employed no counsel, but Mr Ramsay informs me that the other men, who are to be tried, may be benefitted by the cross-examination on mine, which is the first'. Accordingly, Counsellors Bell and Joy were retained, at a fee of £100 each (in contrast to Ramsay's refusal to accept a fee). The outcome was never in much doubt. 'When the witnesses had finished, Russell made his moving speech which the faithful Ramsay carefully reported'; but Russell was condemned to death. Madden, the historian of the United Irishmen, based his account on 'Notes of the Trial of Thomas Russell, found amongst the papers of his Law Agent, Mr. Ramsay of Belfast, obtained from the successors in business of Mr. Ramsay'.

Thomas Garrett, born in 1774, seems to have been younger than Ramsay. In 1808 he married Ann, niece of Samuel Neilson, one of the founders of the United Irishmen, and both owner and editor of the radical (and, on occasions, seditious) *Northern Star*. Neilson, like Russell, was arrested in 1796, imprisoned in Dublin and Fort George, and set free in 1802; he emigrated to America, where he died in 1803.

The firm of Ramsay & Garrett was a substantial one. A ledger for the years 1812 to 1818 survives, and contains much information about the nature of the practice. Ramsay looked after most of the Dublin business of the firm, and there are many entries relating to articles brought or sent by him from the capital to Belfast: 'cash paid for half a pig, £2.4.6'; 'for two bottles of Rose Oil in Dublin, 5/-'; '1½ doz. silver forks, £21'; 'your proportion of Bill due for Rum, £58.2.11'; 'cash paid 2 pairs drawers, 10/-'.

The ledger was beautifully kept by the book-keeper (probably also managing clerk) George Russell Cruise, who delighted in elegant flourishes of penmanship, and especially in drawing little hands with pointing index fingers designating unusual items. He received a salary of £12 10s. a month, and at one point received a present from the partners of £20 16s. 10½d., the exact amount of an inexplicable discrepancy in the firm's books. In addition, there was a senior clerk in Dublin, John Marlow, whose salary was not disclosed to Mr Cruise; William Hackett at £8 13s. 4d. a month; P. F. Webber, who came up from Dublin for five months in the winter of 1814–15 at a salary of £8 6s. 8d., and drew the staggering figure of £260 6s. 7d. 'by cash paid expenses from Dublin to Belfast and back'; Timothy Daly, who was paid £7 11s. a month in 1813 only; G. Gilbert, who was paid £10 a month from 1816 to 1819; and Samuel Robert Griffith, who was paid £6 13s. 4d. a month. The engrossment of deeds and parchments was sent out to George Fitzpatrick, scrivener, who was paid irregularly — he seems to have earned an average income of around £50 a year. Finally, Mrs Woods was employed as office Fire Lighter and Cleaner at the rate of 4 guineas per annum.

Though not all these clerks were employed at the same time, this was still a very large staff for a provincial attorney's office. So late as 1841, the 2,572 attorneys then practising in Ireland employed only 147 law clerks and 87 scriveners between them, according to the census returns. Moreover, in 1813 the firm paid almost £600 to a builder named Thomas Price for a new purpose-built office at 5 York Street, Belfast — unhappily destroyed in the blitz of 1941. Apart from the usual probate and conveyancing work the firm transacted a good deal of commercial business, some of it for clients or correspondents in London, Birmingham, Leeds, Glasgow, and Edinburgh. A number of the local textile firms and bleachers were clients.

There was a run of bankruptcy work after the end of the war in 1815. Local institutions that were clients included the Belfast Insurance Company, the Commercial Bank, the Belfast Accumulating Institution, the Commercial Building Company, and the New Established Traders, in which Charles Brett of Charleville was a partner. There was a certain amount of shipping business; Mr Garrett had to take urgent action on behalf of 'Capt. Thos. Bouch, part owner of the ship of that name' against his partner for £20 9s. 6d. 'passage money for three passengers from this to Quebec whose names had not been inserted in the list of passengers, although they had paid Mr. McCloy their passage money, and sent by him on board'. Proceedings were defended in respect of a consignment of soap condemned in the West Indies. Mr Bradbury, who was laying pipes for the new gasworks, had to be advised of his rights when the 'Belfast Gass Company' failed to pay him. The firm acted also for private individuals and gentry, including Lord Northland. The largest case it had to undertake during the years covered by the ledger was an action by William Tennent against Lord O'Neill to foreclose on mortgages for £6,000, on which interest of £540 was overdue.

Both James Ramsay and Thomas Garrett were plainly men of considerable ability, and the firm prospered. In 1815 Thomas Garrett bought for £2,500 Cromack Farm, a desirable little estate beside the River Lagan on the outskirts of the town – now built over, and known as the Holy Land, from the biblical street-names chosen by the developer. The house was rather a handsome one, the gardens and grounds were extensive, and were prettily delineated in 1818 on a map by Thomas Pattison, which hangs in the office still.

Of his ten children, five boys and five girls, three died young; Henry Garrett, James Ramsay Garrett, and Thomas Garrett all became attorneys and joined their father in the family firm. Robert, the youngest son, became a civil engineer, served his apprenticeship road-making under Charles Lanyon in north Antrim, and was killed at Cawnpore in the Indian Mutiny of 1858 while surveying the line for a new railway. The eldest daughter married Wills Brett; the youngest daughter, Sarah, married a Westmeath attorney of unconventional tastes named Thomas L'Estrange. Old Thomas Garrett died in 1837, aged sixty-three; he too was described as 'an eminent solicitor of this town'; the eldest son, Henry, inherited Cromack Lodge, and the boys carried on the practice, but apparently with only moderate success. The office building in York Street was sold about 1840. At some time in the 1850s Henry Garrett dropped out of the firm, which was thereafter known as 'J.R. & T. Garrett'. As it happened, all three sons were to die comparatively young. James Ramsay Garrett, 'a man of retiring nature' and a more than competent natural scientist and ornithologist, died of fever aged thirty-seven in April 1855, leaving four small children – orphans, for his wife had died before him. Henry Garrett, an individual of literary tastes, married Emma Grimshaw – daughter of one of the firm's most prosperous clients – but died in Dublin aged forty-six in 1859. His daughter had died in infancy, his son became a Metropolitan Magistrate and presided at Bow Street until 1936. Thomas junior, the youngest of the three, died of typhoid aged forty-one in October 1861, leaving a widow and three infant children.

When the younger Thomas Garrett died, his nephew and former apprentice, young Charles Brett, aged only twenty-two, found himself in an unenviable position. He had inherited a somewhat run-down firm, and a measure of responsibility for the support of two widows and eight small children. As if this were not enough, his own father was to die nine months later, leaving him to support also his widowed mother and nine brothers and sisters. It was no doubt with some degree of desperation that Charles Brett appealed to his uncle Thomas

L'Estrange, husband of his mother's youngest sister, to come to the rescue.

L'Estrange, born in 1822 at the home of his grandfather near Mullingar, had been reared by his maternal grandmother at Kilnagarna near Athlone in a literary atmosphere — one of his cousins was Mrs Craik, author of *John Halifax, Gentleman*. He was the nephew, too, of the sinister Thomas Mulock, who was so rude to Wordsworth at Lausanne in 1820, and whom Wordsworth in revenge dubbed Muley Moloch. He was educated at Trinity College, Dublin, with the intention of becoming a clergyman of the Church of Ireland 'but finding himself out of harmony with the doctrines of his church, decided to become a lawyer'. He was accordingly articled to an uncle in Dublin, and admitted a solicitor in 1847. Three years later he married Thomas Garrett's daughter Sarah; he does not seem in his earlier years to have practised his profession, but, until the appeal for help from his nephew, lived the life of a country gentleman in County Westmeath, where he had inherited property.

His arrival in Belfast caused some stir amongst the more conventional citizens. His 'disharmony with the doctrines of his church' was extremely marked. He was all his life a devoted and enthusiastic enemy of organised religion in all its forms. He was a passionate admirer of Shelley, both as republican and as atheist; he was the author of numerous anti-religious pamphlets published by the Rationalist Society in Ramsgate; he scrawled 'Surpliced Ruffians!' at the top of the list of local clergy in the office copy of the *Belfast Directory*; he threw volumes of the law reports down the stairs at the nuns when they came collecting; he scratched out the word 'God' in his books, wherever it appeared, with great neatness and a very sharp penknife. He confided to his younger partner that he could not quite describe himself as a Liberal, as, despite his atheism, his early upbringing had left him with a stronger prejudice against Roman Catholicism than against any other Church.

Thomas L'Estrange greatly admired, and corresponded copiously with, Thomas Love Peacock, whose peculiar style of dry erudition he shared. His own copies of Peacock's books are criss-crossed with annotations and translations of Greek, Latin, Hebrew, German, French, Italian, and Spanish references. He paid Peacock the curious compliment of publishing anonymously, at his own expense, two pirated volumes of Peacock's poems, with local Belfast place-names substituted for the Thames-side topographical references of the originals.

He was moreover an incorrigible pamphleteer: I have succeeded in identifying some twenty anonymous publications from his pen, though I have not traced copies of all of them; their titles include, *Belfast Pygmies*; *The Cyclic Poems*; *Clerical Pooh! Pooh! Rhetoric*; *The Lamentations of Iddo*; and *Creed of a Secularist*.

Plainly old Mr L'Estrange was a considerable eccentric. His unmistakable crabbedy handwriting crops up from time to time on old documents, but I do not think he ever worked very hard in the family firm; I think he rather lent *gravitas* and, no doubt, capital, while his nephew struggled with the work. The *gravitas* must, however, have been suspect at times: he was a sardonic old man with a sense of humour not much attuned to late-Victorian conventions. In his latter years he lived at 7 Howard Street, near the centre of Belfast. It was his custom to stand out of doors, leaning on the railings of his tiny garden, every evening, wet or fine. It is said that a neighbour, greatly daring, eventually screwed up his courage to cross the road one wet night and enquire: 'Tell me, Sir, why do you lean against your railings for half an hour, every evening, wet or fine?' – to receive, after a long pause, the laconic reply – 'To fart, Sir'.

As a colleague in the day-to-day life of the office, he had his disadvantages. Each morning, he used carefully to wrap his chest, back, and arm-pits in blotting-paper below his shirt, lest he catch cold on the walk; and his first act on arriving at the office was to undress in order to remove the swatches of blotting-paper and lay them out before the gas fire to dry. But his relations with his nephew 'Charly' seem always to have been serene and amiable. His home life seems to have been equally happy. Habitual annotator of books, his copy of Oliver Goldsmith's *Works* is touchingly inscribed: 'Sally brought me this book. 1895 Thursday 29 Aug: The last day that Sally appeared to be in good spirits. 1895, Thursday 5 Sept: Sally drove in her carriage the last time, she went to Ballylesson. 1895, Friday 1 November: Sally knew me for the last time. 1895, Monday the 11th of Novr – The funeral of Sally'. And then, below, in pencil: '1900, 9 July: visited her grave'. He himself died at home in 1910, aged eighty-eight, in the middle of the declaration of the results of the general election of that year, which edged out any obituary notice from the local press, with one exception, the *Northern Whig,* which remarked, rather deceitfully, 'in creed he belonged to the Unitarian body, and published a number of books dealing with religious matters'. In 1933 a respectful article in the *Belfast Telegraph* recalled the 'keen-eyed, long-chinned, thin-lipped, silk-hatted old gentleman'.

Several times a year clients will call or telephone, asking to see Mr L'Estrange. 'But it was him I saw last week', they say, in dismay, having mistaken the name, when I tell them he died nearly seventy years ago. It is a form of immortality that I think he would have relished.

THIRTEEN

In 1920 my great-grandfather wrote to his friend Lady Byles: 'The family of L'Estrange is from Westmeath and of the regular old English garrison type. My old partner was very odd in many ways & used to say "don't call me a Liberal. I am bigoted and prejudiced". He was quite emancipated, except that to his dying day he hated a papist'.

'Hated a papist!' How typical, at first glance, of the old ascendancy Irish Protestant; bigoted and prejudiced, indeed. And yet, on second thoughts, Mr L'Estrange was very far from being a typical ascendancy Protestant: for was he not a Shelleyan atheist? This was not just a case of 'If I am an atheist, then I am a Church of Ireland atheist'. I think rather that the old gentleman belonged to that school of thought, widespread in the latter half of the nineteenth century, that hated Catholicism from a purely rational point of view, as the most authoritarian of all the Christian Churches. His position had much in common with the French party of atheism, freemasonry, and anti-clericalism derived from the principles of the Revolution. It was the steady encroachment of the Catholic Church on the freedom of non-Catholics that alarmed the Liberals and radicals: Cardinal Wiseman's pastoral letter of 1850, 'from the Flaminian Gate'; the promulgation of the doctrine of Papal Infallibility in 1870, inexpressibly shocking to the exponents of intellectual liberty; followed by the still more offensive *Ne Temere* decree of 1912. It is possible, in Spain, in Italy, in South America, to resent the pretensions of the Roman Catholic Church without being a bigoted Protestant; or for that matter a bigot or a Protestant at all. But to adopt such an attitude in Ulster is, for all practical purposes, impossible.

The posture of an old-fashioned French atheist is one to which I find myself intellectually attracted, and I might well have succumbed to that attraction, but for two considerations. The first is that almost nobody in Ireland would understand such an attitude; hostility to the Catholic Church is automatically equated with Protestant bigotry. The second, and clinching, consideration is the fact that, throughout the half-century since the partition of Ireland, the Catholic minority has received less than fair treatment from the Protestant majority. So that I often find myself on the side of the Catholics in Northern Ireland affairs, faintly ridiculous as such a posture may seem for a Church of Ireland atheist and an interdenominational anticlerical. It is not as difficult as it would have been only a few years ago, for an increasing number of Catholics are dissatisfied with the way their Church conducts its affairs. It is no longer hard to find pious and committed Catholics in Ireland, of all classes, who for their own good reasons are prepared to have recourse to clerically disapproved methods of contraception; or to send their children to state schools, which the Catholic Church in Ulster forbids.

I think it is of crucial importance to take a very careful and balanced view on the question how far Catholics were discriminated against by Protestants during the fifty-year life of the Stormont parliament. There has been, in recent years, a tendency amongst Republicans to take it for granted that their case is proven, and beyond argument; a tendency amongst Unionists to believe, self-righteously, that the case against them has been disproven by continuing I.R.A. violence after reforms had been extorted. I have said that 'the minority received less than fair treatment' from the majority, and I stand by it. I have not said, and I do not believe, that the minority was actually oppressed by the majority. In 1964, when Catholic discontent at its permanent exclusion from positions of power and authority was beginning to simmer, I wrote a careful analysis of religious discrimination, published in a series of articles in the *Guardian*. I think my conclusions were correct; they have, I think, been borne out by the various inquiries, reports, and White Papers published since then. My conclusion in 1964 was: 'In general, it appears that there is less deliberate discrimination on the part of the Unionist Government than the Nationalists allege; but in the sphere of local government, and in the private sphere, there is far more discrimination than the Unionists will admit'.

The majority of grievances of which Catholics then complained were attributable to an arrogant carelessness on the part of the Unionists, rather than any deliberate ploy to maintain a tyrannical system of rule. The Protestants, after all, had a two-to-one majority in the state; they had little need to act oppressively. Dr A. T. Q. Stewart puts the Unionist case fairly when he writes: 'Though they did not want home rule for Ulster, the unionists made the best of the situation, and contrary to popular Catholic belief, they did genuinely try to create a non-sectarian state in which all citizens would enjoy equal rights'. And: 'In 1923 . . . Sir James Craig . . . met the IRA leader, Michael Collins, in London, and agreed with him that if the operations of the IRA in the north were ended, his government would do everything within its power to protect the lives and property of Catholics in Northern Ireland. This promise Craig and his successors kept'. Myself, I think Dr Stewart slightly overstates his case; some of the speeches and actions of men like Sir Basil Brooke and Sir Dawson Bates take some explaining away. But I think his basic proposition is correct, at least in relation to the first leaders of the new state, Carson and Craig. Unfortunately, their successors were men of less imagination, and failed to realise the need to keep overhauling the system so that it should not fall behind the changing standards of democracy elsewhere. The fight for civil rights came to centre on the demand for 'one man, one vote': an entirely legitimate demand, and a battle in which I played a leading part myself. But few outside commentators realised that this was a battle for justice for its own sake, not for a change that would bring about any substantial alteration in the balance of power. Most Catholics had votes already; the removal of the property qualification in local government elections, the abolition of business votes, the redrawing of boundaries, the modernisation of the electoral laws, were necessary to provide parity with British standards; they would not in fact – and, when they came about, did not in fact – effect any considerable change in the representation of the Catholic community: a minority it was, and a minority it remains.

There were, of course, very real complaints about religious discrimination in the building and allocation of houses, and the distribution of jobs. It was not very difficult to find outrageous examples of Protestant misconduct in both fields. But it was not impossible to find examples of Catholic misbehaviour too. At the root of all complaints of this kind lies the old 'patronage' system, a tradition going back several centuries in Irish history – there remains to this day a very widespread feeling in Ireland that an individual's first obligation is to his co-religionists, that a Catholic should do all in his power to see that a job or a house goes to a fellow-Catholic, and that a Protestant should do likewise. This is closely allied to the 'spoils' system as it works in party politics; the Unionists certainly tended to appoint too many of their own number to profitable offices; but their record compares favourably with that of the political parties in the Republic – there is no more constant refrain in the politics of Southern Ireland than that the party in power is packing the bench with its own nominees.

And some of the wounds suffered by Ulster Catholics were, and still are, self-inflicted. A number of them plainly result from the Church's determination to opt out of the state system of education. Others spring from the reluctance of many young Catholics, less marked today than it used to be, to apply for offices in a system of government that they regard as alien and unacceptable. Some, of course, result directly from the long campaign of violence of the past few years: any employer, Protestant or Catholic, may be excused for hesitating before offering employment to an individual who has demonstrated connections with, or even sympathies for, the activities of the paramilitaries and the murder squads.

Perhaps the most justified of all the complaints of the Catholic minority before 1969 was the failure of the Unionist authorities to accord them fair representation on the numerous public and semi-public bodies that play so large a part in the administration of the community. The statistics are plain and incontestable: Catholics were grossly and disgracefully under-represented on such bodies. But even here, the Catholic sense of grievance went beyond what was justified; there were too many Catholics who chose to opt out, and expressed no willingness to serve; in any case, it affected all non-Unionists, including Protestants of Labour or Liberal views, and trade unionists.

Although I am convinced that the Catholic grievances did not amount to oppression, and certainly did not justify the recourse to force that followed the early peaceful demonstrations of the civil rights movement, I stand firmly by the statement that, in a great number of ways, the Catholic minority received less than fair treatment from the Protestant majority. I think the Unionists could, without the slightest risk to their entrenched positions of power, have met these Catholic grievances with a spirit of fairness and generosity. Had they done so, I do not believe that any of the Troubles of the years since 1969 need have occurred. But perhaps saddest of all, though understandable enough, the Catholic sense of bitterness and oppression has survived and grown, even though the intervention of Britain has produced reforms that, in my view, have met all the legitimate complaints from which the Troubles sprang in the first place.

*   *   *   *

I spent my long vacation in the summer of 1948 in Italy. It was an interesting period; the war was not long over; reconstruction was only beginning; there were almost no tourists; many of the galleries had not re-opened; a general election was in progress. In laborious and archaic Italian (for at Oxford I had been reading Machiavelli and Guicciardini) I questioned everyone I met about the election issues. To almost everyone the choice was a straightforward one – between Communism and the Catholic Church. In that year, the Italian Communist party was at great pains to dissociate itself from Moscow; it appeared to promise a kind of independent Communist state on the Yugoslav model. I went to election meetings in Bologna, and was impressed by the great processions of working men carrying plain red banners through the streets; impressed, too, by their identification with the redshirts of the Risorgimento – the Communist symbol was the head of Garibaldi framed in a red star. The Catholic Church fought under the banner of Democristiana: every street was plastered with posters threatening that a Communist victory would mean *'Divorzio e Libero Amore'* – Divorce and Free Love – symbolised by a tangled nest of serpents. Of the men I talked to, almost all intended to vote Communist; but of the women, almost all intended to vote Democristiana. There are more women than men in Italy, so I was not much surprised at the Communist defeat. But having seen something of the poverty of the industrial towns – the slums of Naples and Bari frightened me more than anything I had seen elsewhere – I thought that I, myself, should (had I been an Italian) have voted Communist. I do not think it was my Ulster background, or my Protestant up-bringing, that made me view the Catholic party with suspicion and distrust; it had about it a tinge of feudalism and indeed of the old days of Peter's patrimony, a faint whiff of corruption, a hint of neo-fascism, and a strong overdose of clerical authoritarianism.

I travelled in Italy partly by train, partly on foot, mostly by hitch-hiking. This could be alarming; it was too soon after the war for British visitors to be made welcome. Several times I met with scowls and blank refusals of lifts or lodging: on one occasion, a party of men in a lorry made me unload its contents single-handed to pay for the lift: they had all been prisoners of war in England, and were getting their own back: so I spent a sweltering afternoon shovelling aubergines, while they sat in the shade and cracked jokes at me. I bore no ill-will, for I had worked alongside Italian prisoners in the potato-fields of rainy Warwickshire, and felt heartily sorry for them. But the experience made me a little careful; I was always glad to accept a recommendation of a lodging-house from any English or American student or visitor met on the roads. It was in this way that I came to the lodging-house kept by

Signora Morandi in Florence: I had been told that she was an Irish-woman, married to an Italian, and that she would always find room for a compatriot.

When I rang her door-bell and asked for a room, explaining that I came from Belfast, she invited me in warmly. Then an awful thought struck her: 'You're not a Protestant, are you?' she asked in a strong brogue. When I confessed that I was, she was greatly taken aback. But, once having taken me in, she could hardly turn me out. She solved the problem by placing me at table with a party of five young Englishmen, all students for the priesthood studying at the Beda College in Rome, and giving them strict instructions to convert me. They rose to the challenge; so did I.

For a week, we wrestled with each other, spiritually and intellectually. They were intelligent young men of my own age. During the days, we mostly went sight-seeing. When dusk fell, and dusk falls early in summer in Italy, we foregathered in the austere dining-room of Signora Morandi's establishment. There, between bony mouthfuls of pesce d'Arno, we disputed, and wrangled, and hypothesised; Mrs Morandi would come at intervals to egg us on — and the debates would continue all night. One day, at my request, they took me to mass in the cathedral and explained to me, in detail and at length, the significance and symbolism of every sentence and every action. That week provided me with an intensive grounding in Catholic theology. I learned a lot. If I have today some grasp of the position of the Catholic Church, I owe it to those five excellent baby priests from the College of the Venerable Bede: and if any of them should read this, I hope he will accept it as an expression of my gratitude.

* * * *

What Irish writer was it who pointed out that, though one may meet liberal and intelligent young priests a-plenty, one never meets liberal and intelligent older priests? If not quite fair, there is an uncomfortable amount of truth in the observation. Certainly, the Irish priesthood as a whole, and more especially the bishops, have a reputation for a sour and restrictive narrowness that extends far beyond the suspicious Protestants of Ulster; extends, indeed, far outside Ireland. And the relationship between Catholic clergy and Catholic laity in Ireland is more puzzling today to an outsider than ever it has been.

The classical Orange view has always been that Catholic Ireland is a priest-ridden country; that no layman dare defy his parish priest; that no politician dare defy the bishops; that through the confessional and the threat of excommunication, the priesthood hold the laity in a grip of steel. It is certainly possible, historically, to marshal a good deal of evidence in support of this view. That Home Rule means Rome Rule has always been a Protestant article of faith: the well-remembered episode when a tentative kind of health service, introduced in the Republic under the name 'Mother and Child Scheme', was quickly withdrawn by a timorous government because the hierarchy considered it an inadmissible interference with family responsibilities, is an example in point. Any layman who presumes to defy the rulings of the hierarchy may expect 'a belt from a crozier', and the mere fact that this phrase has passed into common usage speaks for itself. The attitudes of the Church in Ireland on contraception; divorce; the censorship of books; mixed marriages; above all, the separate schooling of Catholic children, add up to reasonable grounds for Protestant opposition to a united Ireland. If it is oppressive for playgrounds to be locked on Sundays against Catholic children in the north, is it not even more oppressive for the sale of contraceptives to be banned, for the courts to be closed to Protestants desiring divorce, in the south?

Since the days of *Pacem in Terris,* and the second Vatican Council, there has been some relaxation in the rigidity of Catholic attitudes, but the process has not gone far. Valiant campaigners for the freedom to use contraceptives, or for mixed schooling, have been able, not always without difficulty, to obtain a hearing. The rules on abstention at Lent and on Fridays have been greatly relaxed, to the benefit of social intercourse between Catholic and non-Catholic. It is comparatively easy now for a Catholic to attend a christening, or a wedding, in a Protestant church — no easy matter in some dioceses a decade ago. The actual appearances of the churches have changed divertingly: just as Presbyterian churches are more and more abandoning the old Puritan austerity, so Catholic churches are becoming less ornate and more austere: the mass-table has replaced the elaborate high altar and frilly reredos of Caen stone: the mass in English is a much more homely and down-to-earth service than the old muttered mystery of the Latin mass. But on essentials, the Catholic Church in Ireland remains stern and intransigent. A child whose parents send him to a good state grammar school, instead of a bad Church school, may still be refused the sacrament of confirmation; the Declaration on Christian Education

(*Gravissimum Educationis*) of Vatican Two has brought about no change here.

It is hard for a non-Catholic to tell just how and why this comes about. But all Catholic laymen (though possibly rather fewer lay women) seem to be much more liberal-minded than their clerics; very many are prepared to criticise the Church's policies privately; an increasing number are prepared to do so in public. But still, in most cases, the strict discipline of the ranks holds good. Is it in order that this discipline may be maintained that the clergy are so determined in their hostility to mixed education? It sometimes looks like it. Even where younger and less narrowly conservative bishops are appointed from Rome in place of the older die-hards, there seems to be little softening of the regimen. A former Catholic chaplain to the Queen's University of Belfast for a while seemed to be becoming a champion of more liberal attitudes; a belt from the crozier was administered, and suddenly the eminently civilised Monsignor was heard from no more. In 1963 a new younger bishop was appointed to the diocese of Down and Connor (which includes Belfast) in the place of Dr Mageean, a conservative of the old school. Dr Philbin arrived with a reputation for academic distinction, and a love of the arts; a man of mild and tolerant disposition, likely to hold out the hand of reconciliation to estranged fellow-Christians of other denominations. Soon after his enthronement, I made an appointment and went to call upon him privately: as a recently retired chairman of the Northern Ireland Labour Party, I wanted to convey to him the message that not all non-Catholics were bigots; that there existed a non-sectarian party with much sympathy for Catholic grievances against the Unionist state; and that the time was ripe for a coming-together of reasonable and civilised Ulstermen of both traditions.

I left his house feeling saddened, and (for once) cynical. Dr Philbin was courteous and charming: I admired his collection of modern paintings, just as I was later to admire his elegant volume of translations from the Greek anthology: but it was plain that he had been warned to beware approaches from the modern Greeks, even bearing gifts. He had heard, he told me, that the Orange bands actually played their party tunes louder when they were passing the Catholic Mater Infirmorum hospital on the Crumlin Road: he for his part had no wish to be unfriendly, but could I really ask him to extend any degree of co-operation to Protestants if they behaved like that? I reached the despairing conclusion that he had already been 'got at' by the surviving ecclesiastics of the old régime. I think I was right; his attitudes and public pronouncements throughout the years since his elevation seem to confirm it.

It is certainly unusual, it is perhaps impertinent, for a non-Catholic Ulsterman to call the words of the Pope in aid; but I cannot help wondering whether the hierarchy in Ireland has sufficiently digested the words of Pope John, in his opening speech to Vatican Two: 'In the daily exercise of our pastoral office, we sometimes have to listen, much to our regret, to voices of persons who, though burning with zeal, are not endowed with too much sense of discretion or measure . . . . They behave as though they had learned nothing from history, which is, none the less, the teacher of life'.

*   *   *   *

Though the Protestants of Ulster view with (I think) legitimate suspicion the desire of the Catholic Church to impose on non-Catholics its own attitudes to divorce, contraception, and education, there is one other subject upon which they find the attitude of the Church puzzling and ambiguous: its policy towards the I.R.A. If Dr Philbin is prepared to refuse the sacrament of confirmation to innocent children whose parents have sent them to the 'wrong' schools, why is he not prepared to refuse the sacrament of Christian burial to self-confessed murderers? The answer of the Church is that the possibility of last-minute repentance cannot be excluded. This is widely regarded by Protestants as evasive and unsatisfactory. Not many Protestants have acquainted themselves with Catholic Canon Law, but those who have, have noted that – in the absence of some sign of repentance before death – the Church deprives of the right to ecclesiastical burial persons who are excommunicated, or interdicted; those who have committed suicide; those who have died in a duel, or from a wound received in a duel; and 'other public and manifest sinners'. Is not a self-confessed I.R.A. gunman a 'public and manifest sinner' to the Church? Is his sin less grave than tampering with episcopal documents, or presenting a child for non-Catholic education, or getting married before a Protestant minister, or undergoing an abortion on medical grounds? It seems strange to non-Catholics that all these are grounds for excommunication, but homicide, as such, is not. A. T. Q. Stewart has written, 'What has always been noted about the Irish is their capacity for very reckless violence, allied to a distorted moral sense which magnifies small sins and yet regards murder as trivial'. Can it really be true that the Catholic Church in Ireland itself partakes of this 'distorted moral sense'?

The military funeral processions up the Falls Road, the bearer-parties and escorts in smart uniform and black beret, the firing of shots in the air over the graveside, make plain and open the affiliation of the dead man with paramilitary organisations, organisations that the Church has publicly, and repeatedly, condemned. Why then does not the Church employ against these men, and their families, the sanctions that it does not hesitate to impose on children? The conclusion drawn by most Ulster Protestants is that the Church is insincere in its condemnations of violence, murder, and the I.R.A. And I am not sure that they are entirely wrong. Perhaps the most charitable conclusion is that Catholic clerics, just as much as Unionist politicians, are the prisoners of their own laity or electorate: they dare go only so far in condemning views that are widely held by their supporters, lest they forfeit that very support. Yet the niggling doubt remains: if the hierarchy is strong enough to impose on a largely reluctant laity its views on contraception and education, why does it not feel strong enough to impose with equal firmness the views it professes to hold on violence?

*　　*　　*　　*

I have, I think, as many close friends who are Catholics as I have who are Protestants: but then I must confess, most of my closest friends share my own sceptical outlook; and I do not number many very pious people, Protestants or Catholics, amongst my intimates. Yet I hope I can say truthfully that I have abstained from discrimination on religious grounds, not only as between Catholic and Protestant, but also as between the pious and impious. Still, though I try to master my prejudice, I find the somewhat ribald, somewhat anti-clerical, somewhat bohemian party of anti-puritans a good deal more congenial than the earnest, committed, and high-minded. It is the custom in Ulster to paint improving texts on natural outcrops of rock, on the gable-ends of barns, and on the very carriageways. Though diverting in a way, it is also disconcerting: the largest three-dimensional conundrum I know is a slab of rock on the shore of Strangford Lough that enquires, unanswerably, 'Eternity where?' If I were ever to seek to impose a text on my sorely tried fellow-citizens of Ulster, it would be one from the *Notebooks* of Samuel Butler, and it would be to the address of both Catholics and Protestants:

It is all very well for mischievous writers to maintain that we cannot serve God and Mammon. Granted that it is not easy, but nothing that is worth doing ever is easy. Easy or difficult, possible or impossible, not only has the thing got to be done, but it is exactly in doing it that the whole duty of man consists. And when the righteous man turneth away from his righteousness that he hath committed, and doeth that which is neither quite lawful nor quite right, he will generally be found to have gained in amiability what he has lost in holiness.

FOURTEEN

Charles Henry Brett, my great-grandfather, born in 1839, died in 1926, two years before I was born. He must have been a precocious boy; in a youth educated entirely at home, it argues strength of mind that, at the age of thirteen, he should have defied his father's wishes, and asserted his own view of the plausibility of the Thirty-Nine Articles. In autumn of 1852 the sorrowing Wills Hill Brett led his son by the ear (literally or metaphorically) to the office of his uncle Tom Garrett in Belfast, and set him to work to learn the trade of an attorney.

He started as no more than an office-boy; he was obliged to live in digs in Belfast; the years of his adolescence were not happy ones. Twenty years later, he wrote to the father of one of his own apprentices — 'I was a whole year in my uncle's office before I was bound. I served five years almost exclusively at hard work in Belfast, much harder than I ever thought of asking [your] Charles to do, and I spent just as little time as I possibly could in Dublin. The result was that I was, when sworn in, of almost indispensible value to my uncle, and yet the salary he offered me was such as I would not for a moment think of offering [your] Charles. . . . we would propose to pay him £70 a year beginning from the date he was sworn in – This much exceeds what my uncle gave me at a time when (I say without vanity) I was a more useful man in an office'. Some part of his apprenticeship must, of necessity, have been spent about the High Courts and court offices in Dublin. In 1854 and 1855 he attended law lectures at the recently founded Queen's College in Belfast, but as he had not matriculated (for want of prior schooling) was not eligible to take a degree. Long afterwards he recalled that music had been his principal solace: 'At the age of 13 I came to Belfast, when my only musical possession was an old guitar, not a very cheerful instrument, but many a weary hour it helped to pass'. One hopes his landladies thought so too.

When he was twenty-two, his last surviving Garrett uncle died, and the young man found himself obliged to take over the conduct of the firm, with the help of his uncle L'Estrange. The financial complications and responsibilities were considerable. The incoming partners bought the goodwill of the firm from Thomas Garrett's widow for £1,500, payable over six years, and undertook to collect the debts due from clients, less a commission. The estate of James Ramsay Garrett owed the firm over £900, but this could hardly be collected while his orphan children needed the money. The partnership bank account with the Provincial Bank of Ireland had to be guaranteed by the Rev. George Craig, husband of Charles Brett's Aunt Mary (she who had been at school at Avenham in Lancashire in 1815). In return Mr Craig required life-insurance policies to be taken out as security for his obligation; this complicated arrangement led to much friction and unpleasantness. For the first eight years Charles Brett and Thomas L'Estrange divided the profits equally; but it was always understood that uncle L'Estrange was not to be expected to work as hard as his young and energetic nephew, and from 1869 till his retirement he received only a quarter of the firm's profits.

In 1862 the young man's father died, leaving him only £20, and responsibility for his widowed mother, his elder sister, and eight younger brothers and sisters whose ages ranged from twenty-two to eight. The family moved into a rented house at Carlisle Circus, then 'in the suburbs of Belfast'. The early years of practice were plainly full of the gravest financial worries; office commitments could not always be met as they fell due; there was harassment from bankers, from clients, from the firm's Dublin agents, from hard-up members of the Garrett family. Notwithstanding all these office and family preoccupations – or perhaps because of them? – the young man embarked on a very early marriage: in April 1863, when he was not yet twenty-four and she was twenty-six, he married Margaret Neill, daughter of a Presbyterian merchant of Belfast, and set up a house of his own a little further up the Antrim Road. The marriage turned out a very happy one; Margaret Brett (Maggie to friends and relations of her own generation) was a quiet domestic girl, good at cooking (even in the High Victorian age of servants she insisted on making all the sauces and gravies herself over a spirit lamp in the dining room); also at crocheting; sympathetic to her husband's burgeoning interests in law, politics, music, public affairs, archaeology, sanitation, painting, and so on, if not herself in the least interested in any of them.

There were six children, the eldest, Charles Wills, born just a year after the marriage; Alfred (my grandfather) born a year after that; Lucy; Helen; George; and Mary Garrett (Nina to the family). Unhappily the eldest died of scarlet fever before he was three: two rather pathetic memorials to him survive: a very sad (and, I am afraid, very bad) poem by his mother; and a copy of a children's book inscribed 'Papa's London book – Charlie & Affy, 8 February 1867' – the infant Charlie died next day. Charles Brett's commitments to his mother, brothers, and sisters did not decrease as swiftly as his own family commitments increased; his difficult brother Tom, struggling to establish himself as a barrister first in Dublin and then in London, remained an encumbrance until 1870 – 'I cannot go on helping. I have my own family to support, & I have to assist largely in supporting my mother & sisters towards whom not one other member of the family (except George) ever contributed 6d, & in fact altho' I am doing a very good business it often gives me great difficulty to meet my own engagements'. In the following year, the last of the boys having left home, the house in Carlisle Circus was given up and a house was found for old Mrs Brett and the girls at the Crescent, Holywood; that same house where sixty years later I was taken to visit Great-Great-Aunt Mary and her cat.

By degrees the legal practice began to build up. Run-of-the-mill conveyancing work provided the bread and butter business of the firm, but the jam (if any) was provided by commercial work and the more ambitious kind of litigation. In the last year of his apprenticeship, Charles Brett had been involved in the great Belfast Cave Hill case, in which a body of local conservationists (much before their time) succeeded in establishing before Chief Baron Pigot a public right of access for ramblers, picnickers, and pleasure parties, over the path from Greencastle to the Buttermilk Loaney and the Volunteers' Well, and over the whole escarpment of the Cave Hill, which rears itself above Belfast as Arthur's Seat does above Edinburgh. At first the very youthful attorney found litigation too much for him, but by degrees he turned his hand to it, and eventually became an extremely shrewd and experienced practitioner in cases especially involving commercial (or as he himself called it, mercantile) law: patents, trade marks, the early joint-stock companies, partnerships, liquidations, bankruptcies: he was deeply involved in the long drawn out litigation between Marcus Ward & Co., the go-ahead mid-Victorian printers and publishers, and Vere Foster, liberal philanthropist and author. But he came to specialise in the complex legal work required in connection with the establishment of the new railways, which were spreading over the northern counties of Ireland in the second half of the century: this involved the promotion of Parliamentary Bills in London – often opposed by the proprietors of competing lines. In December 1873 he wrote 'I have been so extremely busy for some time past (I am in charge of the promotion of three Bills in Parliament & opposing three others in addition to my ordinary work!) that I have been greatly overworked'. It is sad to have to record that not, one of the brave new railway lines he promoted a hundred years ago is still in existence today.

These frequent visits to London, and to the wider world of Parliament, had a certain glamour, which is lacking from the present day – out on the early 'plane in the morning, home on the late 'plane in the evening. It was the family custom, observed also by my grandfather, my father, and me, to bring back from London some rather special presents for the children; I well remember my first real Winsor & Newton box of oil-paints; I have already mentioned 'Charlie & Affy's London Book'.But for my great-grandfather, and for me also, these trips on legal business afforded opportunities for meetings with those active in politics. The Garrett partners in the family firm had carried on the radical traditions that they had inherited from the days of the United Irishmen; the youthful Charles Brett embraced those same traditions with equal, or even greater, enthusiasm.

In the early 1860s the Liberal Party in Belfast was in a state of some disarray, though in earlier years it had been not unsuccessful. In 1865 a new Ulster Liberal Society was formed, and decided, on short notice and with inadequate prior organisation, to contest one of the two Belfast seats in the General Election of that year. The candidate selected was Lord John Hay, son of one of Wellington's field-marshals and a brother-in-law of Lord Dufferin; the agent was Charles Brett. The campaign was not a success, the two Conservative candidates being elected by a large majority. (Since Charles Brett was to be remunerated for his services, he did not cast his vote, as this would, rather surprisingly, have constituted a corrupt practice under the law then in force.) But the experience was useful, and this was the first of many electoral battles in which he was to engage as 'conducting agent' and, between elections, registration agent. In retrospect it seems at first surprising that a young man so deeply committed to Liberal principles should never have let his name go forward as a Parliamentary candidate. But, at this period, only well-established men of means could afford to do so; certainly a struggling young attorney could not have contemplated the possibility. And by the time Charles Brett could perhaps have taken the risks involved, the Liberal Party had split, and he found himself on the unpopular side.

The uncommonly exciting General Election of 1868 was to be the high-water mark of his electoral success in Belfast. The interregnum since the last election had been put to good use; the Liberal Association was well prepared; but the contest was full of imponderables. In the first place, the franchise had been greatly extended, and there was no way of knowing how the new voters would go. The 'Town Hall Tories' were at this time unpopular with the ratepayers. The Conservative candidates, between whom there was a rift, were Charles Lanyon, a better architect than politician, and John Mulholland, a rich linen merchant (later Lord Dunleath) who was not personally popular. The principal issues were Irish Church disestablishment, and a Land Act to give legislative force to the Ulster Tenant Right. The Liberals chose as their candidate Thomas McClure, a Presbyterian merchant committed to voting for disestablishment, and thereby angling for the votes of the newly enfranchised Presbyterian and Catholic voters: Charles Brett acted as his agent. But the Orangemen, deeply dissatisfied with the Tories, chose as an independent candidate of their own the redoubtable William Johnston of Ballykilbeg. Johnston had recently been imprisoned at Downpatrick for defying the Party Processions Act; he was a fiery Orange Protestant, but at the same time popular with the small farmers since he stood for reforms in the system of land tenure. He was a strange ally for the Liberal McClure: but the alliance was, in the event, to secure the return of both – leaving Belfast for the last time in its history without Unionist representation at Westminster. Johnston was, in fact, a cousin of Charles Brett – Jack Brett, the Downpatrick attorney, had been his great-uncle – and it is conceivable that this relationship had something to do with the alliance.

The campaign was a lengthy one, beset by tortuous negotiations. If Mulholland could be induced to withdraw, Lanyon and Johnston would almost certainly have been elected: but Mulholland refused. If Johnston could be induced to withdraw, Lanyon and Mulholland would almost certainly have been elected. Johnston was having difficulty in raising enough money to finance his campaign; the Tories offered him £2,000 to withdraw, which he refused; as an alternative, they placed obstructions in the way of his fund-raising, with such success that it seemed he might be forced to abandon the fight. At this point the Liberals, through Charles Brett, offered £500 towards Johnston's expenses, and though the offer was officially declined, the money was unofficially accepted. This transaction was to found an election petition, presented early in 1869 by the Tories, to have McClure unseated for engaging in a corrupt practice (not, be it noted, to have Johnston – the recipient of the payment – unseated). The case was an extremely exciting one, and aroused vast interest; Charles Brett was called, recalled, and closely examined as a witness; in the event, Baron Fitzgerald found that the payment was a legitimate one, and declared McClure duly returned. The Liberal victory at this juncture, in Belfast of all places, made the passage of Church disestablishment by a large majority a foregone conclusion.

Despite this not inconsiderable success, Charles Brett declined to act again for McClure 'as I consider he treated me very badly'. I rather think that my great-grandfather expected to receive some appointment to paid office, under the 'spoils' system as it then existed, and was disappointed. In 1872 he sought McClure's support in his application for the part-time post of Clerk of the Crown for County Antrim; he was, in fact, appointed to the inferior office of Clerk of the Peace for Carrickfergus, which he held till its abolition in 1899.

In 1869 he acted as agent for Sir Shafto Adair in County Antrim; the election was an uncommonly rowdy one, though Sir Shafto, a popular and improving landlord, was 'a kind-hearted cultivated man, with all the manners of the old aristocratical Whig school'. In 1872 he acted for Serjeant Dowse in the City of Derry, seeking re-election after his appointment as Solicitor-General for Ireland, this time with success; Dowse, 'always rough and ready', was 'a humourist of a somewhat strange kind', who very soon after accepted a seat on the bench. In 1874 he had a double success, acting as agent both for Thomas Dickson in Dungannon (both men were involved in an unsuccessful attempt to promote a Tyrone Coal Mine Company) and for James Sharman Crawford in County Down; Mr Crawford unfortunately was 'an aged bachelor, in delicate health'; when Mr Gladstone proposed a visit to Ulster in 1877, he intended to stay with Mr Crawford at Crawfordsburn, but the project had to be abandoned as Mrs Gladstone was to come too, and plainly the couple could not stay with a bachelor, however respectable, however Liberal. In 1878 he acted as agent for John Shaw Brown, a linen merchant, in Belfast, but without success. Mr Crawford died the same year: his brother, Major Crawford, stood for the County Down seat in 1880, with Charles Brett as agent; but 'not being a rich man, made it a condition that his electioneering expenses should be strictly limited'. This was unfortunate, especially as the Tory agent made it public that he had infallible means of breaking the secrecy of the ballot; and in the event, Lord Castlereagh polled twenty votes more than Major Crawford. The result was another election petition, vigorously conducted by Charles Brett, which foundered on the invincible dislike of one of the judges (the aged Baron Fitzgerald) for the nominal petitioner, a carman from Newtownards. The two judges disagreed, and the sitting member accordingly got the benefit of the doubt.

In 1885 Charles Brett acted as agent for Robert Murray in East Belfast, but in this election all the nine Liberal-held seats in Ulster were lost; the alliance between the Conservative and Nationalist parties at Westminster caused the Catholic voters of Belfast (and elsewhere) on this occasion to 'vote the Orange ticket'. It was in the summer of the same year that Lord Randolph Churchill also visited Ulster, and used the words that reverberate still – if Ulster is faced with Home Rule, 'Ulster will fight and Ulster will be right'. And it was only a year later that Lord Randolph was to write – 'if the G.O.M. went for Home Rule, the Orange card would be the one to play. Please God it may turn out the ace of trumps and not the two'. This was the last of my great-grandfather's active adventures in practical politics. He had acted as 'conducting agent' in nine Parliamentary elections, and won five of them. In addition, he acted as Honorary Secretary to the Belfast Liberal Association from 1865 till 1874. He had made the acquaintance of a number of the leaders and the coming men of the Liberal Party in England; he corresponded with John Stuart Mill, John Bright, John Morley, and Mr Gladstone himself. A brisk postcard from the Grand Old Man hangs, framed, beside a signed portrait of the writer, in my outer office to this day: 'I thank you for your obliging letter received at Hawarden, and for the apposite and telling extract from the Belfast News Letter, the substance of which I have today recited to a meeting of 3000 persons at Derby. Your very faithful servant, W. E. Gladstone'. He was a member of the National Liberal Club in London. And he formed a friendship with James Bryce, political philosopher and later to be Chief Secretary for Ireland, British Ambassador to the U.S.A., and Viscount Bryce of Dechmont, O.M.

The turning-point in my great-grandfather's political career, and indeed perhaps in his whole life, came in 1886, when he was forty-seven years old. This, the year when Gladstone (on his return from a holiday in the Norwegian fiords) announced his conversion to Home Rule, was a year of heavy import for Ulster: comparable with 1798 (eighty-eight years before) and 1969 (eighty-three years later).

In the immediately preceding years, Gladstone had shown himself emphatically opposed to Home Rule. The violence of the Land Leaguers, the Fenian dynamiters, and the Phoenix Park murders could in his view only be met by successive Coercion Acts. The words 'for ever' in the Act of Union remained sacrosanct. But in 1886 occurred one of those sudden reversals in British policy between coercion and conciliation. Gladstone gave no prior warning to the Irish Liberals, though one of them, Thomas MacKnight, afterwards asserted that strong hints had been given by James Bryce on a visit to Belfast in April 1885: 'Home Rule is coming; take my advice and buy a revolver'. The words themselves are implausible: Bryce was not the kind of man to advise recourse to force in any circumstances: but he may well have had an inkling of the way Gladstone's mind was moving.

In April 1886 Mr Gladstone's first Home Rule Bill was introduced in Parliament – crowds assembled round the newspaper offices in Belfast to buy the latest editions as the details came through on the telegraph. Most Ulster Liberals reacted with a sense of outrage. On the last day of April a monster meeting of protest was held in the Ulster Hall; the final speaker summarised the general reaction: 'He was a Liberal to the heart's core. But Liberal as he was – and Radical if they liked – he would say this, that he was as much opposed to this Bill as any Orangeman in Belfast'. In England, the Liberal party was deeply divided; but most of the rank and file, despairing at the failure of repeated attempts to deal with violence by repression, followed Gladstone's lead. In Ulster, almost nobody – except my great-grandfather – was prepared to do so. The Ulster Hall meeting led to the formation of a committee of 'Liberal Unionists'; but for these former colleagues Charles Brett felt nothing but bitter and derisive contempt. His personal position was the more unpleasant since he had been one of the founders of an Ulster Reform Club, declared open just six months earlier by Lord Hartington, who had used the occasion to express opposition to any project of Home Rule. It now required its members to declare their adherence to the principles of 'Liberal Unionism' and the unfortunate Charles Brett found himself excluded from the club that he had helped to found only a few months before. No wonder that, years later, he was to write to his friend Bryce, 'The Ulster Reform Club party . . . are Liberal Unionists by name, and reactionary Tories in practice'. Thereafter, instead of eating a clubbable lunch in the company of his fellow-Liberals, he was constrained to eat a solitary egg (boiled for him by the apprentice) in the office.

It was not only the Liberals of Belfast who reacted forcibly to the first Home Rule Bill. In previous years there had been serious riots of a party and sectarian nature in Belfast: 2 dead, 4 injured in 1813; 4 dead in 1832; 12 dead, 100 injured in 1864; 5 dead, 243 injured in 1872. But the troubles of 1886 were far more grave than any that had gone before, or that were to come after until the early 1920s (it is estimated that 544 people lost their lives in Belfast in the troubles of 1920 to 1922), and the 1960s. Between May and September 1886 at least 32 people were killed, 370 injured, numerous shops and public houses burned, dozens of families (both Catholic and Protestant) intimidated out of their homes. In the first phase of the rioting, the Protestants of the Shankill Road attacked the police and the army with great violence, evidently believing that Government intended to use them as instruments for the imposition of Home Rule. In this, these troubles resembled those of October 1969, when the Shankill Road turned on the forces of order under a similar apprehension. In the second phase, Protestant and Catholic shot at each other, without interference from police or army, the full length of what is now the peace line between the Shankill and Falls Roads. 'That many lives were lost is generally believed, but if so, the bodies were privately buried without notice having been given to the public authorities'. In the final phase, after Gladstone's short-lived government had fallen, the conflict was between the Catholics of the Falls Road and the security forces.

It was this period of rioting that set the pattern for much that was to follow. Advertisements appeared in the Ulster papers seeking drill instructors, and 20,000 Snider rifles. The disturbances spread outside Belfast. The drilling and arming of private paramilitary armies started. Neither Nationalist nor Unionist doubted that further struggles on the Home Rule issue lay ahead. The vast majority of Protestant Liberals realigned themselves with the Unionists and, in the slightly longer run, with the English Conservative party; the Catholic Liberals were forced into the arms of the Nationalists. It is interesting to note that my great-grandfather seems never for a moment to have contemplated throwing in his lot with the Nationalist Party, even though its leader, Parnell, was an Irish Protestant. For Charles Brett, Home Rule was a means towards liberal reforms in Ireland, not an end in itself. But there was no longer any popular support for a moderate reforming party seeking the votes both of Catholic and Protestant.

Although it was long before he gave up all hopes of living to see better days, such a state of affairs was bitterly disappointing and frustrating to my great-grandfather. It was as well that he had other interests. Indeed, for a man whose only education had been received from his parents in a country parsonage, the breadth of his interests is startling.

Of these the most important, throughout his life, was music. He taught himself, as a boy, to play the guitar; as a youth he took 'a few lessons at the piano'; next he taught himself to master the organ, and was honorary organist of St James's church while his home was on the Antrim Road (he was not a church-goer: it was music rather than religion that took him there). About the age of thirty, he learned to play the cello, and this was his principal instrument for the rest of his life. In 1873 Charles Brett was one of the negotiators for the amalgamation of the two rival musical bodies in the city — the Classical Harmonists' Society, and the Belfast Music Society (in which he sang as a bass) — into the Belfast Philharmonic Society. He remained an active committee member till 1926, and the energetic honorary secretary from 1883 onwards. He played regularly in the Society's concerts, even when he was over eighty. In 1906, in response to a presentation from the members of the society, he 'hoped and believed that music would continue to flourish after golf and bridge had gone out of fashion'. In 1924, the Society's fiftieth anniversary, he received another presentation, and had Sir Henry and Lady Wood to stay with him for the jubilee concert — a performance of the Dream of Gerontius.

But if all his life he was deeply attached to classical music, he had a musical *bête noire*; he detested barrel-organs, which then played regularly in the streets of Belfast. In 1910 he wrote indignantly to the Commissioner of the R.I.C. in Belfast: 'If your men would summon one of the offenders, the nuisance would cease, but today one of these organs played for a quarter of an hour opposite this office, and one of your men, No. 857, walked to and fro enjoying the music instead of doing his duty'. The last of them disappeared some fifteen years ago, and I for my part much regret its passing.

Music was very much part of family life. The children were growing up, and about 1880 the family removed to Gretton Villa South, on the Malone Road, a very large semi-detached red-brick house, recently built by Bass Ratcliffe and Gretton the brewers, with a sunny and private garden. Between 6 and 7 o'clock in the morning of 3 March 1892 the house caught fire; the list of contents in the insurance claim is revealing; it included two pianofortes, two violoncellos, five violins, and two violas. Charles Brett himself and Nina played the cellos; Alfred the piano; George the violin (extremely well); Lucy the viola. Margaret Brett crocheted, and Helen drew or painted, while the others played. Charles Brett was perhaps something of a tyrant as a father; none of the girls ever married, though Nina nearly became engaged to a quite suitable young barrister; it is said that her father could not bear to have the family chamber music broken up, and refused to countenance the match, though he had to resign himself to the marriages of Alfred and George.

Unfortunately, the fire destroyed, not only three of the musical instruments, but many family papers, pictures, pieces of furniture, and heirlooms from Kircubbin, Charleville, and Killough. Alfred and George, who shared a large bedroom, lost everything they possessed; the lists and valuations of their clothes, in their own handwritings, make interesting reading. As well as his clothes – 5 suits and 1 dress suit, £27; 3 dozen linen shirts, £12; 12 pair boots, £12; 1 top hat (new), £1, and one ordinary hat, 10s. – Alfred (aged twenty-six, and a little of a dandy) lost six gold rings; two old swords; a fishing-rod; a stock whip; and a coach horn. The fire damage auction sale realised £28 4s. 2d., ending, most oddly, with 1s. for a fire-damaged mouse-trap. Everything in my great-grandfather's study was totally destroyed; and already he possessed a formidable library. This he proceeded manfully to replace, despite the fact that he had been under-insured, and received only ten shillings in the pound on his insurance claim. His range of reading was extraordinarily wide. He was interested in local history, topography, and Irish literature; so early as 1870 he had written a paper on the topography of Belfast, which I found of much value when writing my own book on Belfast almost a hundred years later. He had a lively interest in archaeology; he corresponded about botany with successive curators at Kew; as for natural history, he extorted from Charles Darwin in 1871 the reluctant admission that he had made a mistake in his description of the breeding habits of snipe. He bought all the latest books in French as they were published in Paris; I have inherited early editions even of writers such as Proust; Professor Savory wrote in 1926 of his 'vast knowledge of French literature, great distinction as a French scholar, and his knowledge especially of French medieval literature'. Towards the end of the nineteenth century he and his daughters interested themselves in the Irish literary revival: they set to learning the Irish language: their shelves were full of the works of AE, Yeats, Synge, O'Casey, James Stephens, and Lady Gregory, as well as the more political works of Horace Plunkett, Tom Kettle, O'Hegarty, and their contemporaries.

As to the visual arts, my great-grandfather was not, I am selfishly sorry to say, a collector of paintings – he was more interested in line than in colour; he liked the book-illustrations of Gustave Doré, Samuel

Palmer, John Flaxman, Caran d'Ache, and Carruthers Gould. But he was energetic in his attempts to interest the Belfast public in modern art. Sir John Lavery and Sir Hugh Lane were both friends who came to stay at Gretton. Indeed, when the fate of the Lane collection was still uncertain, Lane offered Belfast (at the instance of Charles Brett) the opportunity of buying a number of paintings at half price — including works by Vuillard, Corot, Courbet, Berthe Morisot, Fantin Latour, Puvis de Chavannes, Orpen, and Lavery — if only a municipal gallery were established. And these, by present-day standards, were bargain prices — they were catalogued, before his offer, at £800 for the Courbet; £480 for the Puvis de Chavannes; £450 or £150 for Corot; £160 for Vuillard, Fantin Latour, or Berthe Morisot; £35 for the least expensive Orpen. Needless to say, the offer was not accepted. This was in 1906: another attempt was made by Charles Brett in 1908, when as President of the Belfast Art Society he secured guarantees from local businessmen for the cost of an exhibition of pictures, borrowed from Lane in London, in the Central Library. As he remarked at the opening, Dublin now had 'a very fine collection of modern pictures brought together by Mr Hugh Lane', but no adequate gallery; there were now proposals for building a new gallery in Belfast, but no pictures.

No doubt my great-grandfather's interest in art was stimulated by a series of family holidays in France, the Black Forest, and Italy, from each of which were brought back books, prints, reproductions, and miscellaneous antiquities of a modest kind. In 1894 Alfred (who had been ill) and Helen set off on a leisurely three-month holiday in Egypt, from which they brought back many more curios, and an illustrated travel diary. Helen was a more than competent artist both in water colour and in oils; she and great-grandfather experimented also in wood-carving. Gardening was pursued with great seriousness, and cousins in England were instructed to post toads in perforated tins to Gretton at suitable intervals; these were then let loose in the orchid-house to rid it of noxious insects (cloports, slaters, or wood-lice in particular) — toads being, like snakes, unknown in Ireland. The girls, as they grew up, interested themselves actively in various suitable charitable bodies. Alfred attended Queen's College, qualified as a solicitor, and joined his father as a nominal partner (though very much a junior one). George too served his articles as an apprentice in the office, but it was felt that there was not really room for all three of them in the firm, so he was packed off to Dublin to qualify and practise as a barrister; he eventually became moderately successful, but until he was over thirty, required more financial support from home than was convenient. Nevertheless, the years between 1880 and 1914 were pretty prosperous.

Apart from the Philharmonic Society, Charles Brett took a lively interest in housing, sanitation, public health, and the Belfast transport system – he preferred however to walk the four miles or so from his home to the office. In 1900 and the succeeding years, he wrote a number of sardonic letters on municipal subjects to the papers under the pseudonym 'Senex'; at this period affairs in the Belfast Town Hall were more than ordinarily corrupt, and he took considerable pleasure in castigating the Conservative-Unionist aldermen and Councillors. In 1906 a Vice-Regal Health Inquiry 'was visited on the city through representations made to the Chief Secretary, James Bryce, by the leading Liberal, Charles Brett; Professor Byers of Queen's College;' and the Citizens' Association.

From 1908 to 1911 he chaired a committee carrying out an unofficial investigation into sweated labour amongst the handkerchief embroiderers of Counties Down and Donegal. Here, his contacts with Augustine Birrell, the Chief Secretary in Dublin Castle, and Lord Aberdeen, the Viceroy, came in useful: a Board of Trade Inquiry was instituted as a result. This committee brought him into contact also with the early labour and trade-union leaders of the north, and he was content to work in alliance with them on social and economic questions, much as he disliked socialist politics. One of these allies was Mr Mallon, secretary of the National Anti-Sweating League, who told the Belfast Trades Council that 'ever since he arrived in the city, he had seen on the hoardings that the wages of sin is death, but when he took up the papers he saw that the wages of virtue was three farthings an hour', which he thought 'hardly a sufficient distinction'.

In 1906, to his considerable surprise, Charles Brett received a knighthood from Campbell-Bannerman's government. The news reached him from his old friend James Bryce, the Chief Secretary.

The honour was pretty well received in Belfast, even by Unionists, though it was felt to be unexpected in the case of someone who had taken no active part in politics for two decades. Numerous letters of congratulation were received, and carefully filed away. One or two of them were a bit gruff in tone; Francis Joseph Bigger, Nationalist antiquarian, wrote 'I am sufficient of an Irishman to believe that the honour is the other way, but no matter'; Dr Anthony Traill, Provost of Trinity, red-hot Unionist, and now Alfred Brett's father-in-law, wrote stiffly 'It is right that your services should be recognised when your party comes into power'; old Thomas L'Estrange, sardonic as ever, wrote 'Dear Charley, At the risk of being thought unbusinesslike I venture to offer you my congratulations on your upward step on the social ladder', and devoted the rest of his letter to business matters. Various congratulatory addresses were presented by the bodies with which Sir Charles had been associated; to one of these he replied – and I think his reply is not just a piece of pomposity, but rings true –

> I can truthfully say that I am not of an ambitious nature, but I have one very strong aspiration, and that is, that my name may be remembered for a while as that of one who desired to be a good citizen of the city where many generations of his ancestors lived and his own life was spent; and who, in the larger affairs of that city, strove to render some little service in the culture and refinement of its civic life.

I shall be pleased enough if, when I reach the age of sixty-seven, I may be able to say the same.

Pleasant as the honour was, my great-grandfather's remaining years were to be embittered by the course of events in his native province. The Liberal reforming government of 1906 had won the General Election by a landslide, and had no need to rely on the votes of the Irish members at Westminster. Home Rule had been, in Parliament at any rate, a dormant issue since the House of Lords had thrown out Gladstone's second Home Rule Bill of 1892. But in 1910 Asquith's new Liberal government, with a much reduced majority, needed the support of the Irish party if it was to force through its Parliament Bill, curbing the obstructive powers of the House of Lords; and the price of that support was a new Home Rule Bill.

The violence of the reaction in Ulster surpassed all the predictions of English politicians. My great-grandfather watched, helpless and with growing horror, the course of events: Winston Churchill's disastrous meeting in Celtic Park: the convention of 100,000 Unionists at Balmoral: the Ulster Covenant, signed within a few days by almost half a million people; the formation of the Ulster Volunteer Force: the gun-running to arm the new paramilitary forces in Ireland, north and south: the Curragh 'mutiny': the temporary submergence of the Home Rule issue in the outbreak of the Great War: the Rising in Dublin of Easter 1916: the Battle of the Somme in July 1916: the post-war negotiations for an Irish settlement: the passing of the Government of Ireland Act;

the Treaty; the Civil War; partition; the establishment of the new Parliament of Northern Ireland and the new High Courts in Belfast; the
Troubles that continued to beset the unhappy country for the rest of his
life.

To some extent my great-grandfather relieved his feelings during
these last twenty years by the letters, sometimes several a week, that he
wrote to his friend Sir William Byles, a Liberal M.P. with a particular
interest in Ireland, and after his death, in 1917, to his widow. Some 200
of these letters survive. They make, on the whole, painful reading.
Their author was aged seventy-four at the outbreak of the Great War,
eighty-seven when he died. He was unable to adapt his views and his
opinions to the terrible events of these years, and who shall blame him?
Some of his judgements and comments are of striking ineptitude; his
prejudices had only gathered strength with the years. But some of his
comments, perhaps, are worth quoting.

2 July 1916: 'Thank you for your thrilling description of the Casement trial . . . I have no respect for Casement, who had all the
combined meanness and vanity that he confused and seemed to glory
in. . . . If he said manfully "Yes I am a traitor and I glory in it" I could
have some respect for him, but his aim was to save his skin by any
legal quibble. I hope however he will not be hanged although he
richly deserves it, I think no one should be'.

7 September 1917: 'Joe Devlin gave a dinner party to which many of
the Unionists went . . . a friend who was there told me nothing
could be better than Devlin's conduct and tact. I was not asked but I
got a message afterwards that he intended to ask me but forgot! I am
glad he did, for I feel completely and permanently on the shelf '.

27 December 1919: 'You ask what I think of Ll.G.'s Irish scheme . . .
I think it is entirely unworkable, and I am inclined to think it will
never be embodied in a Bill. The idea of a wire fence separating, say,
two halves of County Tyrone with a different set of laws on each side
of the fence! It is too absurd, and it is clear that the common sense of
all parties revolts from it'.

2 January 1920: 'The talk here is that the Tories are going to work
their new Parliament for all it is worth and they are already looking
out for a site for the Parlt. House. (There will be some glorious

jobbing and robbing). But the real fun is this – The Tory lot comprises Episcopalians and Presbyterians, the latter in a considerable majority – Now it is said that the Presbyterians are going to take completely the upper hand: keep all the fat jobs and patronage and let the other party take its proper, inferior position. . . . This is a delightful prospect to a looker-on like me, and I do hope they will fall out! . . . In fact, politics apart, the two sects hate each other like true Christians'.

25 July 1920: 'The death roll here, 14 at least and numerous casualties, do not seem to affect anyone except the immediate friends of the victims. It seems that the years of war have brutalised or benumbed the public conscience'.

10 July 1921: 'Last night at about 1 a.m. I heard coming from Falls Road – not two miles as a crow flies – at least 100 rifle shots & I fear there was sad work done. It was horrible to listen to it in a civilised (?) country. Our local politicians are true Bourbons and I fear they will, if they can, put an end to any fair settlement'.

20 November 1921: 'I have no influence with anyone of this Government & do not wish to have any – I am also sure that they look on me as an old fogey crank – But I do not care, I never did & never will bow my knee to the Orange idol'.

3 September 1922: 'I am glad the Dail is to meet soon. The new men seem to be capable and I hope they may be able to restore order but it will be a difficult task. Childers' career shows him to be a man devoid of principle. They say his wife is his evil genius. What is your opinion of her?'

25 January 1926: 'Rumour today is that someone else has been shot. I knew poor Redmond who was so cruelly murdered – a fine fellow, and brave to recklessness. . . . But I do wish Sinn Fein would repudiate the murder gangs. They certainly should – but I suppose they are, as Parnell was, afraid'.

Of course the letters of these years deal with many matters other than events in Ireland; family matters, English politics, literature, music and art, the Great War. Many of them express anxiety about his grandson

Charlie, my father, who had gone straight from school to join the Connaught Rangers, and to the trenches in 1916. Sir Charles made a gesture of semi-retirement in 1919, retired as a partner in 1925, but continued to come to the office almost daily until his last illness. In 1921 he was awarded an honorary degree of LL.D. from the Queen's University, an honour that, being without a primary degree, he accepted a little testily. He became increasingly crotchety. He greatly disliked the new-fangled telephone, which had been installed (but not in his own room) before the war, and never mastered the workings of the handle that had to be wound to attract the attention of the operator. He was to be heard, frantically winding the handle back to front, shouting into the mouthpiece – 'Miss! Miss! Come and take this damned machine away!' He became much irritated by small things; my father recalls an occasion when a fly, buzzing about his face in the private office, infuriated him. Before going out, he ordered his senior clerk, William Bennison, to kill or catch the fly during his absence. My father watched with interest. Mr Bennison was not flustered. He walked slowly to the high standing-desk at which he worked, took from a drawer one of the dead flies that he kept ready in stock for such occasions, placed it neatly in the centre of a square of white blotting paper, and laid it exactly in the centre of my great-grandfather's desk.

Sir Charles Brett died, after an illness of a few months, at Gretton, on 17 July 1926, aged eighty-seven. My three great-aunts lovingly pasted the numerous and lengthy obituary notices into a black-bound book, bought for the purpose.

FIFTEEN

It seems to me, as I look ruefully back, that in one respect at least my own career to date has been a mirror-image of that of my great-grandfather. As a young man he threw himself into radical politics, full of idealistic optimism that a new generation could bring reason and enlightenment to the Ulster scene. Just so did I throw myself into Labour politics in 1950. He brought great energy and commitment to the struggle, and for a while it looked as though success was in sight. I thought the same in the early 1960s. But then the old divisive forces of Irish politics reasserted themselves; the delusive interlude of liberalism and toleration came to an end; the conflict was no longer between progress and reaction, but once again between the British-Unionist-Protestant tradition and the Irish-Nationalist-Catholic tradition. After twenty-odd years of active engagement in Liberal politics, from 1865 to 1886, my great-grandfather acknowledged defeat in his mid forties. After twenty-odd years of active engagement in Labour politics, from 1950 to 1969, I acknowledged defeat in my early forties. Not without bitterness, he diverted his considerable energies and abilities to the encouragement of the arts, and especially music; and to various forms of public service at one remove from party politics. Not without bitterness, I too have interested myself in the encouragement of the arts, especially architecture and conservation; and in housing.

If both of us failed to persuade our fellow-countrymen to our own ways of thinking, it was at least, I think, an honourable failure. In our differing ways we helped to keep alive the struggling tradition of reason, tolerance, and civilisation that survived the defeat of the United Irishmen in 1798, and still remains a fragile element in Ulster life. Perhaps its day will come, though certainly not now in my lifetime. Not all the seeds which my great-grandfather sowed fell on stony ground; and I have seen a surprising number of the reforms for which I called in my political days brought to fruition, though by others. Perhaps most important of all, we neither of us ran away. Too many people see the solution to Ulster's problems in terms of running away: those Republicans who think all would be well if all the 'Brits' were to go home, taking the descendants of the seventeenth-century settlers with them; those Unionists who think all would be well if all the 'Teagues' and 'Fenians' were to remove themselves across the Border to the Republic that they admire: those European commentators who advocate an Algerian solution, and the repatriation of the English 'colons' and 'pieds-noirs': worst of all, those English people, politicians and others, who think that decent Ulstermen should have abandoned their homes to the murderers and the paramilitaries. There can, of course, be no solution by mass repatriation. As well expect the American-Irish to relinquish their homes to the surviving Red Indians; descendants of the Vikings to return to Norway, and of the Normans to return to Normandy; the Huns and Goths and Vandals to go home to Siberia. Small-scale emigration has done enough harm already: it is the best young people who, despairing of Ulster, go off to Canada or New Zealand, or merely England, to make a new life, and leave their own home much the poorer for their loss. But, leaving aside the matter of attachment to one's own soil – and, for my part, I think I am as deeply rooted as any man may well be – there is one other and conclusive factor: to leave is to be defeated. The people of Ireland emigrated only when the economic pressures of the Famine became wholly intolerable. The Highland clearances left some of the people of Scotland with no practicable alternative to emigration. The people of England did not rush to emigrate in 1940, or at the time of the Blitz. It is not mere obstinacy, it is a proper self-respect, which makes it unacceptable to abandon one's home at the instance of criminal gunmen.

*   *   *   *

Just as the Liberal cause was in disarray in 1865, so the Northern Ireland Labour Party was in disarray in 1950. For years it had been swithering on the border issue; it had fared disastrously in the general election, fought on that issue alone, of 1949; in the same year, the party conference took the sensible decision to accept partition so long as an electoral majority in the north wanted it, and in consequence the Republican (and mostly Catholic) minority seceded from the party. It had no members of either the Westminster or the Stormont parliament; the secession apart, the older generation of experienced Labour politicians decided that, in altered circumstances, the time had come to retire; a new and younger generation had therefore the opportunity to step in and frame new policies and a whole new approach to the intricate politics of Ulster.

My first few years were spent in the basic grind of work at constituency level. I endured the tedium of 'writing' election addresses — long hours spent transcribing names, addresses, and numbers from the electoral registers; disputing and debating on trivial points of tactics at branch meetings; and, of course, canvassing, which I always enjoyed. It was not very long before I was elected to the Executive Committee of the party, and there, by degrees, I came to be entrusted with the drafting and preparation of policy statements and election manifestos. I have read, with some amusement (it is like sitting in heaven, twangling a harp and reading one's own obituary), an academic thesis on the rise and fall of the Northern Ireland Labour Party that describes me as one of the Party's 'political ideologues'. There is truth in this; but it did not absolve me from the more down-to-earth obligations of membership. I learned, not without difficulty, to speak in public and in the open air; though I was always, I think, too much of a highbrow to appeal much to my audience. I spoke on the Custom House Steps, traditional rendezvous of the left wing in Belfast. On May Day I spoke on the blitzed ground in High Street (long since built over) from the traditional platform, Billy Maginness's cart: Billy was a street trader of very left-wing views who boasted that his horse and cart had provided a platform for every leading politician of the left since the earliest days of the Spanish Civil War. In these attempts at speechifying, the good advice of David Bleakley was invaluable to me. And they were not wholly unsuccessful: on those early May Days, a part of our audience always comprised special branch policemen, sent along by Lord Brookeborough's government to report whether we were, as was expected by the Unionist establishment, preaching both republicanism and treason; I well remember the day when one of these plain-clothes policemen, whose faces we had got to know well, came over to me at the end of the meeting and confided that he and 'all the boys at the barracks' had been convinced, and were on our side.

But I was more at home in a committee-room than on the back of a cart or a lorry. And it was as an 'ideologue' (loathsome sobriquet!) that I had most to contribute. I came to be chairman of the party's policy committee, a post I held (not without challenge) for some fifteen years. I was draftsman of numerous documents, usually in collaboration with Sam Napier and Tom Boyd. The three of us formed, I am afraid, a sort of inner clique within the Labour party, so far as policy was concerned; and this gave rise to considerable friction in later years with some of the other leaders of the party, especially those who had gained seats at Stormont. Between 1950 and 1960 our primary concern was to divert the battlefield of political conflict away from the old sterile plains of border and religion, towards the economic fields of prosperity and employment. In this we were unexpectedly successful. In the Stormont general election of 1958 the party won four seats; at the time, the Unionists were almost incredulous. I shall remember all my life a curious little party, held late at night in my own room in my office, because of its proximity to the City Hall where the count had taken place, when a handful of his friends and supporters celebrated Tom Boyd's success in the Pottinger constituency. Optimistic as ever, I had bought a bottle of champagne beforehand; there is still a dent in the ceiling of my room, perceptible only to the eye of affectionate recollection amongst the scars of bomb damage, where the champagne cork hit the roof. Tom could not be persuaded to sip the champagne: but he shared with the little party of us the belief that perhaps a new day had dawned. And it was not his fault if it failed to do so: of all my colleagues of those days, he was and is the one I most respect and admire. As leader of a tiny parliamentary party at Stormont, he demonstrated by shrewd, steady, level-headed hard work how constructive a constitutional opposition could be. But, though he was recognised as leader of the opposition by the Speaker, the Unionists were less generous, and treated his contributions with their customary off-hand contempt. Indeed, Brian Faulkner, when Unionist Chief Whip, let Tom Boyd know of his intention that no amendment on any subject emanating from the Labour opposition, whatever its merits, would be accepted.

We had already, at that time, hammered out a series of practical policies, which were, in the end, to leave a mark. We had called for direct state participation in the establishment of new industry; that is today government policy. We had called for an industrial development corporation; today the Northern Ireland Development Agency performs almost exactly the function we then envisaged. I am particularly proud of a document entitled 'Rents and Houses', which I wrote in 1956, advocating public ownership of all rented housing accommodation, and private ownership of all other houses; a rent-rebate scheme; security of tenure for public-authority tenants; and an improvement in the quality of new houses. The policy statement contained the sentence, for which I was much teased – 'Diogenes lived in a barrel: but he did so of his own choice'. In 1964 the policy was refined to call for the establishment of a single housing authority for the whole of Northern Ireland, employing a points scheme to avoid political and religious discrimination in the allocation of new houses. In 1970 just such a body formed part of the package of reforms introduced by James Callaghan as Home Secretary; when it was set up I was appointed by the Unionist Roy Bradford one of the first members of its board; of which I remain a member as I write. Here, I have been more fortunate than my great-grandfather. It is not often given to a young man of under thirty to advocate, while in opposition, the establishment of a new kind of institution; and to have confided in him, while still in opposition and still under fifty, a share in the task of setting it up and carrying it into effect. For this stroke of fate, I am profoundly grateful: my experience has been at least to this extent less frustrating than that of my great-grandfather: and if the Northern Ireland Housing Executive should fail in its duty to provide a fair housing service, of good quality, administered with absolute impartiality, for the people of Northern Ireland, it will certainly not be for lack of effort or commitment on my part.

Until at least 1962 our efforts were devoted to establishing a position as a credible alternative party to the Unionists. That meant, unavoidably, that our primary appeal must be to the more reasonable and liberal members of the Protestant majority. But this was the period of the I.R.A. campaign of 1956 to 1962. It was not, by present standards, a campaign of great virulence; but it was sufficiently disturbing; and of course it brought into question the validity or otherwise of the security apparatus with which the Unionist state had equipped itself. This centred around the Special Powers Act, conferring powers of detention without trial, of search, and of arrest, not ordinarily available to peaceful democratic governments; and the employment of the 'B' special police force, an all-Protestant body recruited largely from the Orange ranks, which was in some ways the lineal descendant of the black-and-tans. During this period, some 300 incidents of violence took place, and six R.U.C. men were murdered. This was indeed bad enough; but the significant fact was that the Catholic population of the north declined to rally to the support of the I.R.A. In consequence, the campaign fizzled out. The importance of this sequence of events cannot be over-estimated: it amounted to a declaration, by an overwhelming majority of the Catholic population of Ulster, that it was now prepared to forget the old hostilities, and explore the possibility of peaceful co-operation within the partitioned state of Northern Ireland. This situation was in part brought about by the Catholic acknowledgement of the higher standard of living, and the superior social services and benefits, available in the north in comparison with the Republic. It was a development that should have been welcomed with open arms by the Unionists; at last, it opened up the possibility of creating a state that enjoyed the loyalty and adherence of every section of the population. Of course, some concessions to the Catholic community would have been required to give permanence to this new alignment. Very unhappily, the Unionists were too deeply steeped in their own distrust of the minority to reciprocate: no concessions to the minority as such were forthcoming.

* * * *

This was the state of affairs when the elderly Lord Brookeborough stepped down, and Captain Terence O'Neill took his place as Prime Minister of Northern Ireland. There seemed hope that new men would mean new measures; for the first time, we had a Prime Minister whose opinions had not been formed by the events of 1912 to 1922; in the south, De Valera retired from the premiership to become President of the Republic. I remember giving great offence to Mr Erskine Childers, himself later to be President of Ireland, at a debate in Trinity College, Dublin, when I suggested that we could all start again now that the decks were being cleared of the old diehard generation.

It seemed that, in the north, everything depended on Terence O'Neill, today Lord O'Neill of the Maine. He is a man of wit and charm, but his premiership was lacking, as it turned out, in determination and consistency. In an interview given to the *New Statesman*, in 1958, when he was Deputy Prime Minister, he came as close as any Unionist politician could do to welcoming the advent of Northern Ireland Labour as a constitutional opposition, and a possible alternative government; but, once in power, he refused to accord the party's M.P.s recognition as the official opposition; and in the General Election of 1965 he personally campaigned against the Labour candidates with more energy than he devoted to most other causes. While in office as Minister of Finance, he committed the lapse of judgement of accepting a directorship of the Ulster Bank: yet only a few years later he led a campaign to eliminate conflicts of business interest from Stormont politics, and in the process dismissed a popular Minister of Agriculture for failing to adhere to protocol. He was, as Minister of Finance, a generous friend to the National Trust; but he could nevertheless make a speech of disconcerting ineptitude at the opening of Springhill House, in which he appeared to praise the Trust as a reactionary body devoted to preserving the traditions of landed property and feudalism. When Prime Minister, he surrounded himself with a team of personal advisers from whom he seemed inseparable: Malley, Black, Bloomfield, Montgomery, Roberts; all civil servants, not all of equal calibre, and very deeply resented by O'Neill's political colleagues — themselves a sufficiently mixed bunch.

Under this new management, the subject-matter of Ulster politics changed. There was a new restlessness within the Catholic community; afters its rejection of the I.R.A., many of the more moderate men felt the time had come to abandon the old hard-line nationalist tactics, and seek to play a positive part in the running of the state for the good of all. The younger Catholics, and especially those newly qualifying from the grammar schools and university, were becoming openly impatient at the second-class status accorded to them by Unionists of the old school. There were hopes that O'Neill would meet these wishes; he dropped hints that he would like to do so, if only his own party would let him. To his credit, he did accord recognition to the Northern Ireland Committee of the Irish Congress of Trade Unions, despite the opposition of almost all his Unionist colleagues; and he did invite Sean Lemass, Prime Minister of the Republic, to visit the north — though no business of any substance was discussed between them. But there, for all practical purposes, his adventurousness ended. O'Neill was so shaken by the hostility of the vocal minority of Protestants that he declined to venture further, even though the overwhelming support he received in the General Election of 1965 amounted to a popular mandate for a policy of détente. But it was too late to draw back, or even halt; expectations of reform had been aroused, and could not now go unsatisfied. From 1965 until the explosion of 1969 matters went from bad to worse; the pressure was building up, but O'Neill felt himself unable to meet it. It must be a matter for debate and individual judgement whether, if he had defied his own backwoods supporters, called a snap general election on the issue of reforms, and won it (as I believe he would have done), he could not still have saved the day. He has argued strongly in his autobiography and elsewhere that it was impossible for him to do so. It is, of course, easy to be wise after the event. But it was my judgement then, and it is my judgement still, that even if some of his own Unionists would have deserted him, an overwhelming majority of the electorate at large would have supported him in a policy of reform. I do not want to be uncharitable to an amiable man who behaved honourably according to his own lights, but I firmly believe that with stronger leadership, perhaps with better advice, O'Neill could have saved us all the bloodshed and turmoil of the years since 1969; and that his failure in leadership was the *causa causans* of our present Troubles, and of the troubles that must still lie ahead for many years to come.

*   *   *   *

Between 1963 and 1968 Sam Napier, Tom Boyd, and I fought a desperate and uphill battle to engineer reforms that would avert a return to sectarian violence. This would, in any event, have been no easy task for a small party in opposition; it was in fact rendered even more difficult by the internal division within the party. David Bleakley and Billy Boyd, as M.P.s sitting for hotly Protestant constituencies, though personally much in favour of reforms in principle, thought it ill-judged and premature to take any steps that risked alienating hard-won Protestant support. The majority, of whom I was one, considered that the time had come when the party must actively champion Catholic minority rights, if the possibility of a stable and non-sectarian community was not to be thrown away for ever. But this was a path that needed to be pursued with much delicacy. If we shouted too little, we should forfeit the support of those moderate and constructive Catholics who were now willing to join the party, despite its commitment to partition, in substantial numbers. If we shouted too loud, we should arouse Protestant fears, which had been half-dormant, and precipitate a speedy return to the politics of violence. Our only feasible tactic was to seek to procure reforms by oblique pressures on Terence O'Neill, by private meetings, or through the Labour government that had come to power in Westminster in October 1964.

Within a month after the return of this government, a deputation went to London to press upon Harold Wilson, the new Prime Minister, the urgency of exerting such pressure for reform upon O'Neill. Its members received a sympathetic hearing, but secured no promises. In 1965 I was the principal draftsman of a policy document, 'Electoral Reform Now', that was to become one of the cornerstones of the whole civil rights movement. It is interesting to note that every single one of its major recommendations had been accepted, under duress indeed, before devolution ended and direct rule succeeded it. In April 1965, just after the publication of this paper, the Home Secretary, Sir Frank Soskice, visited Ulster, and we did not miss the opportunity to press him to press O'Neill for urgent reforms. But this was the first of a series of rebuffs; O'Neill had succeeded in convincing the Labour government of his reforming intentions, and instead of exerting pressure on him to go faster, Soskice made a speech at Stormont expressing admiration for his administration.

As 1966 progressed, it became plain that sectarian feelings were rising. There was trouble from Dr Paisley in the spring; there was a build-up of emotion surrounding the fiftieth anniversary of the Easter Rising of 1916; in June there followed the 'Malvern Street murders', first sign of a serious resurgence of Protestant paramilitarism. In September the Labour Party and the trade-union movement jointly addressed a paper on Citizens' Rights to Captain O'Neill: again, I was the principal draftsman of that document: again, it was to be used later by the civil rights movement: again, the demands contained in it have since been conceded. But at the time, it met with a disdainful reception. In December a joint deputation went to press its claim at Stormont Castle – O'Neill was ill, and the deputation was received by four cabinet ministers (Brian Faulkner, William Craig, William Fitzsimmons, and William Morgan), all at that time hostile even to the timorous programme of reform that O'Neill might have been willing to contemplate. This was one of the most depressing meetings I have ever attended; none of the four ministers evinced the slightest glimmer of comprehension of the points we were trying to make, or of the fears that underlay them.

Throughout the previous year we had been attempting, with increasing desperation, to convey a warning to British Labour Ministers, but with little more success. We had bombarded those with whom we had more than a nodding acquaintance with copies of our two documents; I had spent several days in London, lobbying, amongst others, Lord Gardiner, Lord Longford, and a number of influential back-benchers; amongst the few people who were prepared to listen to what we were saying, and take it seriously, were George Thomas (now Speaker) and

Alice Bacon, successive Ministers at the Home Office with responsibility for Northern Ireland. But their advisers, like most English politicians, believed (because they preferred to believe) that the state of affairs in Northern Ireland was bound to improve so long as it was left alone, and so long as Captain O'Neill (charming and reasonable man) was left to bring in reforms at his own pace. The Home Office officials were not only unhelpful, they were downright obstructive, and we had grounds for believing that they were secretly furnishing Stormont with reports on our private representations to Labour Ministers. One of the latter, a most pious and ecumenical Christian, told me: 'This is the twentieth century, not the seventeenth century, and it is just not possible to believe that the religious divisions of Ireland could lead to violence ever again'.

The most interesting, if not the most rewarding, of these meetings took place in November 1966, when Tom Boyd, Sam Napier, and I met Roy Jenkins (by then Home Secretary) in the Home Office. I had high hopes of this meeting: I greatly admired Roy Jenkins both as politician and historian: I knew that, alone amongst contemporary politicians, he had a thorough grasp of twentieth-century history, including Irish history, especially of the period before and after the Great War. I still have my notes for that meeting. We warned him that reforms must come soon if an explosion was to be avoided; that Terence O'Neill was simply drifting, in the mistaken hope that the climate was improving; that the Labour Government should speedily exert every pressure at its disposal, direct or indirect, to secure reforms, and that if its pressures failed, it should be ready to resort to direct legislation over the head of Stormont. I remember that I personally added, as an afterthought, that the Government would be well advised to abandon its support for O'Neill, who was feeble and unable to carry out his promises, even if he really meant them, which must be doubtful; and should instead support Faulkner against O'Neill, as a man capable of carrying his party with him: a bigot, as he then appeared, but one with whom a deal could be negotiated, and one who could carry out what he promised. Roy Jenkins appeared to be fascinated at the suggestion that reforms were most likely to be secured, and bloodshed avoided, by supporting the 'bigot' against the 'moderate'. Plainly, the proposition intrigued him intellectually, and we discussed it up and down at great length. But in the end it became unhappily plain that one lesson he had derived from his study of Anglo-Irish relations in the early years of the twentieth century was that any English politician who touched Irish politics was doomed; he ushered us out more than courteously, but it was plain that we need hope for no help there.

In 1967 there was something of a lull before the storm. No bombs, no bullets that year: somebody threw an empty bottle at the Queen, and somebody else dropped a half-brick on her car, during the royal visit in July; I remember being irritated to the point where I might nearly have thrown a tennis ball myself by the possessive and patronising way in which the Unionist Party treated her as their own private property. A party of Paisleyite clergymen threw snowballs, not in the Christmas spirit, at Mr Jack Lynch, Prime Minister of the Republic, in December. Politically, the year was spent by the Labour Party in attempts to establish a Council of Labour for Ireland. This was an interesting, if up-hill, task: four parties were involved, and their interests were far from identical. The Irish Labour Party, in Dublin, was understandably reluctant to enter into any alliances north of the border, which might alienate its own supporters. The Republican Labour Party in the north, led by Gerry Fitt, considered itself as the natural ally for the Irish Labour Party. The Northern Ireland Labour Party, seeking to establish itself as a non-sectarian alternative to the Unionists in the north, sought anxiously for an understanding with the Irish Labour Party on cross-border matters, while reluctant in the extreme to accord any recognition, however indirect, to its Republican Labour rivals. The Irish Congress of Trade Unions had a legitimate interest in the outcome of the discussions but, not being a political party at all, was bound to tread warily.

A series of meetings took place, some in Belfast, some in Leinster House; as one of the Northern Ireland Labour Party representatives, I took an active part, particularly in the drafting of the non-committal and lawyer-like communiqués. The Irish Labour Party delegates were Brendan Corish – polite, reticent, and unenthusiastic about the whole idea – Sean Dunne; Frank Cluskey; Mick O'Leary; and Brendan Halligan. With these last two, the youngest and least diehard of the party, I formed a very friendly relationship: as also, in the event, with Gerry Fitt, till then regarded in Northern Ireland Labour circles as suspect in the highest degree. It was enlightening to discover that, in a *vice versa* kind of way, politics in the Republic were subject to sectarian and constitutional restraints that were the obverse of those in the north; it was cheering to discover that, there also, there were young radicals impatient with the whole system; and it was highly salutary to discover that Gerry Fitt and his colleagues were human after all, despite the gulfs that divided us. Politics may be a very serious matter, and indeed a very tedious one, but humanity does sometimes break in. I learned that Gerry Fitt, Joe Sherrie, Mick O'Leary, and Brendan Halligan, assembled in the back room of a Dublin pub, amounted to the very best of company; just as I had already discovered that Paddy Devlin, despite his invincible predilection for the automatic epithet 'fucking', was better company than most in the back room of the St John Bosco club in Belfast.

In the end, we hammered out between us a shaky kind of alliance, and a wobbly kind of constitution for a Council of Labour for Ireland; and indeed, had times been happier, it might have achieved something, if only by virtue of the friendly personal relations the negotiations brought about between the participants; but alas, it was overtaken by the terrible events of the following year, and to the best of my knowledge no proper working meeting was ever held. And more, I think, the pity.

*   *   *   *

The Troubles of the 1960s and 1970s began, properly speaking, on 5 October 1968. There had been all too many ominous symptoms earlier in the year. Leadership in the struggle for reform had passed away from the Labour Party to a number of more aggressive bodies (in particular the Civil Rights Association) prepared to take the risk of violence involved in any campaign of public demonstrations. In June Austin Currie dramatically squatted in a house at Caledon that had been allotted to a single girl aged nineteen, a Protestant, in preference to a Catholic family with children; and was in due course equally dramatically evicted by policemen, one of whom was the lady's brother. In that same month the Labour Party made one last attempt to persuade the British government to intervene: I led a deputation to see Lord Stonham, the Minister at the Home Office then responsible for Ulster, and (according to the historian of the Northern Ireland Labour Party) 'expressed forcibly my fears for a revival of sectarian strife unless the genuine grievances of the Catholic community were quickly rectified'. No response was forthcoming; a couple of days later I reversed my previous position and supported the call for a Royal Commission, which till then I had opposed on the grounds that it must lead to a polarisation of sectarian attitudes.

On 5 October there took place the Civil Rights rally in Derry at which, for the first time, the protesters actually broke the law. Gerry Fitt, Austin Currie, a number of members of the Civil Rights Association, and a sprinkling of members of the Northern Ireland Labour Party made to break through a police cordon; the police used their batons; when the marchers retired, they were batoned again by a second line of police. Rioting followed; petrol bombs were used for the first time that weekend; the possibility of a peaceful solution was at an end. On that Monday, when petrol bombs were first flying, the Executive Committee of the Northern Ireland Labour Party sent one final memorandum – of which, for almost the last time, I was the draftsman – to Harold Wilson:

> If the present situation is allowed to develop, and it cannot fail to develop if the Unionist government adopts an intransigent and unyielding stance, there will be a reversion to the Catholic–Protestant hostilities of the 1920s. We are disappointed that the Labour government has not intervened in Northern Ireland affairs. Most members of the labour and trade union movement have gritted their teeth and soldiered on, continuing to place their faith in constitutional methods though in a mood of increasing pessimism. But, as Labour ministers have been warned repeatedly, pressures have been building up irresistibly, and many non-Unionists, especially amongst the younger men, now feel that constitutional means have failed and that unconstitutional methods are justified.

In November 1968 a second joint deputation from the Labour and Trade Union movement went to see Terence O'Neill and his cabinet colleagues, bearing a document beseeching him to accept the principle that British citizenship ought to confer equal citizens' rights in every part of the United Kingdom. We received a chilly reception. O'Neill hinted that we were only concerned about 'getting into the act'; Stephen McGonagle reacted to this with violent indignation; I warned O'Neill, for the last time, of my judgement that, unless concessions were made quickly, the younger and more volatile section of the Catholic community would run out of control; O'Neill replied, stiffly and with hostility, that he regarded this as a threat, and was not willing to be blackmailed.

In January 1969 unarmed civil rights marchers, students for the most part, were ambushed and attacked at Burntollet bridge, on the road from Belfast to Derry; one of the most shameful episodes in the whole history of Irish Protestantism, and one of the most disastrous in its consequences. In May 1969 I declined to let my name go forward for re-election to the Executive of the Northern Ireland Labour Party; and so, for all practical purposes, retired from politics: though I allowed my name to remain on the books of the Labour Party until after the Ulster Workers' strike of 1974, when it seemed to me that the party had irrevocably abandoned the policies of non-sectarianism, and irrevocably identified itself with the Protestant cause. A dozen times since then I have been reproached by friends in the British Labour Party, one at least today a cabinet minister, with the words: 'Why ever did you not warn us of what was coming?' I have never yet succeeded in finding words adequate to reply to that question.

SIXTEEN

Gretton, Sir Charles Brett's home, remained quite unaltered for thirty years after his death. After his widow died in 1930, aged ninety-three, his three daughters lived on there. As a schoolboy, I was taken often to visit my great-aunts: they were kind, hospitable, and friendly, but no longer young. This, like Tennyson's Lotus-land, was a land where it was always afternoon; there was a constant tinkling of tea-cups, and an endless stream of lady visitors, some wearing fur tippets, almost all wearing hats with large hat-pins. There was an annual children's party in the garden, with a treasure hunt involving parcels hidden at the end of criss-crossing clues of coloured string (Aunt Nina's admirably laby-rinthine invention). There was a raucous green parrot in the kitchen, and an elderly and itchy Airedale terrier called Barney. There were beautiful scrapbooks, and wooden bricks, and a china bird with its beak wide open, which could be fed an astonishing number of ivory coun-ters; there were Chinese puzzles and painted boxes-within-boxes; I am glad to say that most of these enchanting Victorian toys are still in the family. When I grew older, I was sometimes allowed to read in my great-grandfather's sunny study. It was not quite a haunted room, but it had a definite and personal atmosphere of its own: very still and silent: faintly scented with the leather of chairs and book-bindings, and an elusive odour of long-ago tobacco. Everything in the room remained exactly as great-grandpapa had left it; except that Aunt Nina, who kept the books dusted and the furniture polished, tried to keep the library up to date with new books, and meticulously maintained the card-index catalogue.

Aunt Lucy, the oldest of my great-aunts, I remember best as a very old lady indeed. Her bed had been brought downstairs to the morning-room. Her face was wrinkled but benign, her hair was silv-ery, she wore a lace mob-cap with a blue ribbon, and round her shoulders were wrapped layers of creamy shawls. She was the literary one of the sisters, and when I was about twelve she presented me with her very own copy of the *Oxford Book of English Verse*, which I treasured greatly. Aunt Lucy died in 1948 at the age of eighty-two.

Aunt Helen was the artistic sister, and she was pleased to have a great-nephew who was interested in pictures. When I was about fifteen, she decided the time had come to give up painting, and presented me with all her gear — tubes of pigment, palettes, easel, and (best of all) an enormous collection of paint-brushes of the very best quality: I use them still. Though she was very kind to me, it must be admitted that there was a certain sourness about Aunt Helen: she could be spiteful, especially to her younger sister Nina; she had a long pale face of which I am always a little reminded by Tenniel's illustration of the White Queen transmuted to a sheep. She died in 1957, aged seventy-nine.

If Aunt Helen was sheep-like, Aunt Nina was undeniably bird-like — a small alert person with a beaky nose, beady eyes, and an inimitable way of cocking her head to one side. As the youngest of three sisters, she came lowest in the pecking-order, as she was very well aware; but perhaps because of this, she was the one of the three best able to make a child feel at home. She was the musical sister, and my lack of interest in (or talent for) music was a disappointment to her, but it made no difference. She was in many ways a childlike person, and in her old age she reverted to her childhood. One day in the 1950s, when she had gone into Belfast on an errand, she took the bus home, not to Gretton where she had lived for seventy years, but to the house on the Antrim Road where she had been born. Quite soon, her return to childhood became so complete that there was nothing for it but a mental home. There she lived out the rest of her life, peaceably and not too unhappily, passing the time in unravelling tangled hanks of string: no present from a visitor gave her more pleasure. She died in 1964, aged ninety-two.

Their brother George, barrister in Dublin, had died in 1938 at the comparatively early age of sixty-seven, leaving a widow and five children. After the death of Aunt Helen, with Aunt Nina already in hospital, the household at Gretton had to be broken up. The contents, and the residue of my great-grandfather's estate, fell to be divided amongst the children of Alfred — my grandfather — and George. The clearing of the house, in which I helped my father, was a formidable task. Almost nothing had been changed since the refurnishing after the fire of 1892. From every drawer, from every cupboard, tumbled the evidences of a world that had disappeared. Here were my great-grandfather's clothes — socks, underwear, 'personal effects' in the most personal sense of the word. And there, his papers; the vast collections of notes and jottings and correspondence of a long and busy life. I think, now, perhaps too many of the latter were burned: but the task of reading and sifting them would have taken years. Thanks to the kindness of my father, uncle, and aunts, some of the family furniture, and a great many of my great-grandfather's books, came directly to me. And when the house had been cleared, there were still precious flowering trees from the Gretton garden to be transplanted . . . It then seemed to me, and in a way it really was, the final closing of a part of the Victorian era.

*　　*　　*　　*

Alfred Brett, my grandfather, born in 1865, lived under the shadow of his father until he was over sixty. Not that he was a nonentity; far from it; but still, he was unable to compete with Sir Charles on the latter's own ground. He went to school at the Belfast Academy, under Reuben John Bryce; he took his law degree at the Queen's College, Belfast, in 1888; served his apprenticeship in the family firm; and was admitted a solicitor in 1891. He was then nominally taken into partnership with his father. His name indeed appeared on the notepaper: but he took no share in the profits, receiving only a fixed salary of exceedingly moderate amount; and was allowed no say in the control of the firm's affairs.

He was, I think, rather a dashing young man. His clothes, his hair, his moustache, were always fashionable and well tended. His interests were outdoor rather than indoor: though he was not ill-read, and played very nimbly on the piano, he liked shooting and loved fishing. These arts he learned from his cousins the Willsons of Drumcroon, the descendants of his grandfather's elder sister Mattie. And in 1896, at the age of thirty-one, he contracted rather a dashing marriage, with Harriett Traill, of Ballylough. She was an exceptionally good-looking young woman – even in old age, she was uncommonly handsome – high-spirited, determined, and an individualist. She came of a county family from north Antrim, of Scottish descent, which had produced (and was still to produce) a number of characters of high and wilful eccentricity; her father added intellectual distinction to the common stock – he became Provost of Trinity College, Dublin, in 1904, and was one of the leaders of the southern Unionists, landlords, and churchmen. The town liberalism of her husband's family was thoroughly alien to her background and upbringing; and she was never a one for making concessions: so the marriage, though not unhappy, was a fairly tempestuous one – especially as my grandmother's tastes were on the extravagant side, while my grandfather's means were, for most of his life, distinctly modest.

The young couple first set up home in a house they called Erinagh, in Comber, County Down, where my father was born in 1897; then in a yellow-brick villa in Osborne Park, Belfast, within a mile or so of Gretton. Three younger children were born: my Uncle Wills Hill, my Aunt Chris, and the baby of the family, my Aunt Barbara. In the office, my grandfather dispensed shrewd advice to those younger clients who were prepared to consult him rather than Sir Charles; though he was incapable of drafting even the simplest will or deed himself, he could criticise constructively the work of others, and his advice as a man of affairs was usually extremely sound. From politics, on the whole, Alfred Brett abstained; like his father, he belonged to the National Liberal Club in London; professing to be a 'Liberal Unionist', he steered a judicious middle course between the political opinions of his own and of his wife's families. He was an active layman in the Church of Ireland, and one of the founder committee members of the National Trust in Northern Ireland.

In the Great War, as a man in his fifties, he served in a territorial unit that guarded the Belfast docks. He watched with quizzical interest, but took no part in, the events surrounding the establishment of Northern Ireland and the accompanying Troubles. Soon after the end of the war he leased a large and rambling eighteenth-century house with Victorian additions, Richmond Lodge, on the Holywood side of Belfast. Several fields went with the house, so my grandmother was able to keep horses, which accorded much better with her view of life than the suburban villa off the Malone Road. Here my grandparents lived in some style until 1941, when the house suffered a direct hit from a German land-mine. Fortunately nobody was hurt. They then removed to Clare Park, an old house perched on the cliffs by Ballycastle in north Antrim, where I spent a memorable summer holiday with them in 1942, watching the north Atlantic convoys sliding across the far horizon between Rathlin and Islay. They ended their long married life in a house at Craigavad, near the south shore of Belfast Lough.

Though I remember him with affection, I went in considerable awe of my grandfather. He was still senior partner when I came to serve my apprenticeship in the firm; indeed, he came into the office every day until his ninetieth year, attributing his longevity to his policy of getting away from his wife for part at least of every day. His rather long snow-white hair was always beautifully brushed, his white moustache neatly clipped; he smoked an occasional cigarette in a long holder; he used his hands to great effect to punctuate his conversation. He had a very sharp tongue, and a great fund of lore, much of it scandalous, about our colleagues, our clients, and all the Belfast personalities of his day. His accent was of a kind no longer to be heard – a sort of educated-Irish brogue. He was never at a loss for the *mot juste*, and never averse to embroidering a good story. Indeed he had, within the family, a reputation as something of a Munchausen, since his claim to have seen tigers in the forests of Jamaica. He had travelled considerably – he and my grandmother always taking their holidays separately. On several occasions he took leisurely passage in a cargo-boat to the West Indies; on one occasion he paid a visit to his cousins in New Zealand, returning around Cape Horn; he was also much given to fishing holidays in Ireland, Scotland, or the Orkneys. My grandmother's holidays were more of the horsey, hunting kind that she had learned to enjoy in her country girlhood at Ballylough. In her last years, when she could no longer ride, she would still follow the hunt on foot, rolling under those barbed-wire fences that she could not climb over.

My grandfather died, in his ninety-first year, in 1955. My grandmother survived him by ten years. Having lived up to the limit of his income all his life, he left an extremely modest estate; he would have chuckled, I think, to hear the wiseacres of the legal profession in Belfast admiring his adroitness in minimising the death duties payable on his demise.

*   *   *   *

My father, after a spell as a day-boy at the Royal Belfast Academical Institution, was sent to Trent College in Derbyshire, which he hated. He left school in the summer of 1914, and that autumn sat his matriculation exam for Trinity College, Dublin, staying in the house of his grandfather, Provost Traill, then ill and dying. Though he passed, the Great War was to deprive him of university education. That same month, he joined the 3rd Battalion of the Connaught Rangers at Kinsale. The Colonel of the 1st Battalion was a friend of his mother's; neither he nor his parents were particularly anxious that he should join the Ulster Division, recruited largely from Carson's Ulster Volunteer Force.

Of his years in the army, my father has written his own account; though he has not sought to publish it, there is a copy in the Public Record Office of Northern Ireland. His first two years were spent in training in Ireland. After the Easter Rising of 1916 he formed part of a flying column under orders to march to Wexford and discourage the 'rebels' who were seeking to take control of Enniscorthy; which it did without undue incident. In September 1916, at the age of nineteen, he was ordered to France to join the 6th Battalion. He was to fight in the trenches, on and off, for the rest of the war; he was wounded twice, the second time in the face at Cambrai in November 1917, and received the M.C. for his part (as a company commander) in the battle. He was still recovering from his wound in England when his battalion was almost wiped out by the German advance of March 1918. He rejoined the reformed battalion in the summer of that year, and took part in the final battles of the war. The Armistice was declared while he was travelling to rejoin his unit after four days' leave in Paris. He was demobilised in January 1919, and returned straight home to Ulster.

He was at once apprenticed to his father in the family firm. After partition, and the establishment of a separate Law Society in the north, it was still necessary to attend lectures in Dublin. Sometimes my father travelled down on his motor-bicycle, but this became hazardous when the irregulars took to stringing wire across the road at neck-height in the hope of beheading black-and-tans. More often he travelled down by train. He saw the Four Courts burning; he saw the Custom House on fire; he saw soldiers and their horses wandering dazed in the fields beside the railway line at Goraghwood when the troop train, carrying the cavalry escort for King George V's opening of the first Parliament of Northern Ireland, was derailed near the border. My father was the first person to sit his final examination for admission as a solicitor under the new Law Society of Northern Ireland: 'I sat by myself in a back room in McGonigal's office in Rosemary Street, for two days, entirely without supervision – a fortnight later Charlie Thom, one of the Law Society examiners, casually met my father in the street and told him that I had duly passed my final – and that was all I ever heard'.

Having been admitted, my father was employed in the firm in 1923 at a salary of £150 a year. 'In 1925 I wished to marry, and asked my grandfather for a rise, and he allowed me £500 per annum. He retired at the end of 1925, and then my father and I entered into partnership, two-thirds to him, one-third to me'. My mother, whom he married in 1926, was half English, half Irish: her father, a 'physician and surgeon' in Leeds, came of an old Yorkshire medical family: her mother had been a Miss Richardson, one of an extensive clan of Quaker linen merchants, settled in Ulster since the seventeenth century. They set up house at Holywood, County Down, where I was born at 12.30 a.m. on 30 October 1928. (My own wife is also half English, half Irish.)

Times were hard, in the office and elsewhere. The Troubles of the 1920s, followed by the great depression, meant that there was little enough work to go round. The unpopularity of my great-grandfather's politics had alienated many clients and potential clients; his hold on the business of the firm had weakened; too much of the work was entrusted to the managing clerk, who was drinking heavily on the sly, and eventually had to be sent away, leaving much neglected business to be attended to. The firm's bank account was shaky, and my grandfather had been too long under his father's domination to know how to set about putting things right. It fell to my father to pull the firm round, which he did with great energy, good humour, and success. By the time the Second War came, he had successfully re-established its reputation and prosperity.

After the war, when I myself in turn had qualified, my father treated me with great generosity. He was determined that one piece of history should not repeat itself, and that he would not overshadow me as my great-grandfather had overshadowed my grandfather. I was immediately admitted to partnership; and comparatively soon thereafter, my father handed over to me his own room and chair, and removed himself to the back room, which was to be totally destroyed by the bomb of 1972. He is today a consultant, and, at the age of eighty, comes into the office on one day each week.

SEVENTEEN

Some resolution, if not solution, of the present Troubles of Ulster there must eventually be, but it is not yet in sight. It has been an extraordinary experience to live through a period so eventful, when so many shattering changes have taken place, and yet so little has changed fundamentally. The sequence of events has been bewildering, difficult indeed to remember: I doubt if many Ulstermen could without prompting give an accurate chronological account of even the major happenings. The fall of Terence O'Neill; the fall of James Chichester-Clarke; the fall of Brian Faulkner; the fall of Stormont; Sunningdale; the Assembly; the Convention; William Whitelaw; Merlyn Rees; Roy Mason. The rise of the I.R.A. and the splits between Provisional I.R.A., Official I.R.A., and the I.R.S.P.; the rise of the U.D.A. and the splits between conflicting paramilitary bodies – U.D.A., U.V.F., U.F.F., and a dozen more. The Battle of the Bogside, and Free Derry corner; the burning of Bombay Street, and Farringdon Gardens; the introduction, and the abandonment, of detention without trial; the introduction, and the abandonment, of special status for 'political' prisoners; Bloody Sunday in Derry, Bloody Friday in Belfast. The loyalist bombing of water and electrical installations; the republican bombing of pubs, shops, offices, homes; the selective assassinations, the random sectarian murders; rent strike; Ulster Workers' Council strike; Action Council strike; squatting, intimidation, knee-capping; torture as revolting as any in history. Constant apprehension, heightened at times to immediate fear, and for some people, to moments of utter terror. Out of the Easter Rising, wrote Yeats, a terrible beauty was born. No terrible beauty has been born, or is likely to be born, out of the Troubles of Ulster.

Yet the great majority of the people of Ulster are decent, kindly, and – in their personal relations as individuals – tolerant. They try, as best they may, to carry on a cheerful social and family life despite the horrors around them, and for the most part they succeed. Traffic accidents still cause more deaths and injuries each year than do the Troubles. Where do the assassins and the bombers come from? They are in our midst, and some of them may well be unsuspected acquaintances.

Of those charged and convicted, proved guilty beyond any remote possibility of doubt, who by way of confirmation refuse to recognise the Court or shout 'up the U.D.A.!', many have been modest individuals whose friends and families would have sworn them innocent. It is perhaps true that the resurgence of both republican and loyalist paramilitaries in 1969 arose from fear, and that both were (in those early days) primarily defensive in intention. I say 'perhaps', for there is on each side a thread of fanaticism leading back to the troubles of earlier generations. It is demonstrably untrue, though some Englishmen still believe it, that the recourse to violence in Ulster springs directly from high unemployment, bad housing, and low earnings. Other parts of the British Isles, including Eire, have conditions as bad or worse. So long ago as 1836, a shrewd observer, quoted by Dr A. T. Q. Stewart, pointed out that the worst violence occurred, not as one might expect, in the poorest parts of Ireland, where economic conditions were harsh, but in the fertile and more affluent regions. Of the bigots, fanatics, and gunmen on both sides, many come from middle-class homes and comfortable surroundings. By no means all are ill-educated: the distorted idealism of the young intellectual, sometimes a revolutionary of the left, sometimes a reactionary of the right, provides the paramilitary armies with more, and more dangerous, recruits than the thick-headed vandalism of the back streets. It is also untrue, though some Irishmen (and especially middle-class Dubliners) still believe it, that this is a war of national liberation, heroic freedom fighters for the national cause challenging a régime of brutality and oppression.

There can be no doubt that, by now, the paramilitary bodies on both sides are offensive, not defensive, in character. Each represents a small minority, even within its own Protestant or Catholic community, grimly determined to impose its own desires for the future structure of society upon co-religionists and those of the opposite party alike. Each has embarked upon a long-drawn-out guerilla war of attrition, in which neither total defeat nor total victory seems possible. Protestant leaders call loudly, sometimes hysterically, for stronger action against the I.R.A.; they are seldom specific about the kind of action they want, except for the perennial call for the return of the death penalty. The strong implication is that they want a return to the methods of the black-and-tans or the 'B' Specials, a kind of all-Protestant militia that would deal ruthlessly with the minority, on the assumption that every Catholic is a republican at heart; and every republican is an I.R.A. sympathiser at heart. That kind of solution cannot be contemplated by anyone who looks beyond the short term. I.R.A. leaders call loudly for the withdrawal of British troops, of British organs of government, and by implication for the wholesale ejection of the Protestant majority who wish to retain the British connection. That kind of solution cannot be contemplated either. What alternatives are left? It is no longer realistic to ask the Catholic community to reject the gunmen in their midst, as happened in the 1950s; nor to expect the Protestant community to reject its own gunmen; for the apparatus of fear, and of revenge, has established too strong a hold. The posture of the Peace Movement deserves respect and admiration, but it is hard to see how it can prove effective. There remains the highly hypothetical alternative of reconciliation – I hardly expect to live to see a reformed (could he be reformed?) Dr Paisley walking arm-in-arm through Donegall Square with a reformed chief of staff of the Provisional I.R.A. There are perhaps other alternatives, some of them not very plausible; there remains the possibility that the Troubles will ultimately sputter to an end through the sheer exhaustion of all parties. I think this may possibly come about; but, if it does, it will leave the underlying conflicts unresolved, with not merely the probability but the near-certainty that the same battles will have to be fought out all over again by the next generation of Irishmen; and the next; and the next.

One of the most surprising features of recent years has been their failure to throw up any real leaders. One might have expected that, even within so small a population, a few individuals of real stature might have emerged from such turmoils. This is the more surprising, since the advent of television seems to lend itself to the growth of personality politics. Yet there were personalities of staggering significance in Irish politics before television was invented; Dan O'Connell, Gladstone, Randolph Churchill, Edward Carson could impose their attitudes on ordinary people in their thousands without the aid of cameras, microphones, or make-up. But on the Unionist side, Enoch Powell is certainly no Carson; Dr Paisley, despite his spokesmanship for a certain strand of Protestantism, and despite a certain resemblance in thick-throated physique, is no Craigavon. On the Catholic side, Gerry Fitt, Paddy Devlin, John Hume, or Bernadette MacAliskey, none of them measures up to the Wee Joe Devlin of the preceding generation. I am not sure whether one should dread, or should hope for, the appearance on the Ulster scene of an individual of comparable stature. A 'bad' leader might lead us from the frying-pan into the fire; a 'good' leader might lead us out of the morass in which we are bogged, by some untracked path that nobody else could discover. But I doubt if Ulster will find a leader, good or bad, now.

This absence of leaders reflects, in part, the splintering of old alignments that the Troubles have brought about. The old sour Nationalist Party, last souvenir of the days of Parnell, is dead and gone; no great loss. The old monolithic Unionist Party has fragmented, its place being taken by a bewildering spectrum of all-Protestant parties united only by their bigotry: no loss at all; one of the few silver linings to the cloud of the Troubles has been the deflation of the arrogance with which unionists used to treat non-unionists. The Northern Ireland Labour Party, to which I devoted twenty-odd years of my life, has for all practical purposes disappeared. So has the Communist Party. The old Liberal Party, to which my great-grandfather devoted twenty-odd years of his life, has altogether disappeared. Sinn Fein, as the political voice for the Catholic gunmen, is overshadowed by its military wing. The S.D.L.P. may yet attract substantial numbers of liberal-minded non-Catholics as well as moderate Catholics; that is still to be demonstrated. The Alliance Party is estimable as, what its name implies, an alliance of reasonable Catholics and Protestants against bigots and extremists: but, though it is plain enough what its members are allied against, it is not so clear what they are allied in support of; and it runs the risk of following the same fate as several middle-of-the-road predecessors. The pattern of the future remains unclear.

Like many another, I find myself in the wilderness. I know with certainty that I bear a share in the blame for what has happened in Ulster during the past decade. My children, and their children, will hold me and my generation responsible for what went wrong; they are well entitled to do so. And yet, what else could I have done, should I have done? I held the opinions that I held: for that matter, I hold them still: they proved unacceptable to my fellow-citizens, the electorate, and that leaves me helpless. I know now exactly what my great-grandfather meant when he said, in 1906, that he had been debarred '*by invincible circumstances*' from taking any leading part in the larger affairs of his native city. Like him, I see nothing for it but to devote my surplus energies to the practicalities of housing, conservation, and the arts, leaving politics to others. And yet there is an inconsistency in this. Here stand I, officiously telling my compatriots that there must be a change of heart both amongst Protestants and Catholics before the problems of Ulster can be resolved. Should I not, in justice, search my soul, and embark upon a like change of heart myself — whether to become a loyalist, or a republican, or an alliancer? I have searched my soul, and I cannot do so. I belong to a generation that failed. It is better, I think, to retire – gracefully if I can, gracelessly if I cannot – and allow the next generation of Ulstermen to discover such resolution of the enigma as they can. I think that solution will be a long time in coming.

*　　*　　*　　*

Many Ulster people (though I think not a majority) seem to want a return to some form of local devolved government. For my part, I am more than apprehensive: in theory, local democracy is fine, but in practice I fear that it would lead irrevocably to a new disaster. To begin with, there is an irreconcilable conflict between those who demand a return to straightforward Protestant majority rule, and those who demand some institutionalised system of power-sharing. It is hard to see how that conflict is to be overcome: but perhaps means may be found. What then? If the Catholic minority is once again to be permanently excluded from a share in the government of the country, though protected by some kind of bill of rights, those who are irreconcilable now are likely to remain so. On the other hand, the fate of the last power-sharing Executive holds out little promise for the future; not that the politicians who took part in it failed to work together – from that point of view it was extremely successful – but the violence of the Protestant upsurge expressed in the U.W.C. strike, the intransigent determination of the majority to concede not even a fraction of its ascendancy, bode ill for any similar scheme in the future. And in my view, such is the depth and intensity of the inter-sectarian bitterness to which the past few years has given rise, that neither party can be trusted to govern fairly. It is in the nature of things that the most extreme candidates, certainly on the Protestant side, are most likely to be elected. Such people, if returned to positions of power, would be too likely to abuse that power. When the unionists are prepared to allow a Catholic councillor, once in a blue moon, to become Lord Mayor of Belfast; when ostensibly 'representative' bodies are ready to elect Catholics to a significant proportion of the posts of influence, instead of arrogating all positions to Protestants by use of the block vote; when Sunday opening ceases to be an issue in the local council-chambers;

then I may change my mind. And there are too many in the Catholic community who might be no better: the loyalists of Ulster might well have reason to fear revenge for past wrongs. There is need for the Catholic leaders to accept that the reforms of recent years have fairly met their former grievances. And there is an urgent need for the Catholic Church to emerge from its entrenchments and show greater willingness to fraternise.

I think that, for the foreseeable future at any rate, direct rule is greatly preferable to legislative devolution. Ulster needs to be treated as an integral part of a larger democratic entity, though it may offend both Irish nationalists and Stormont-minded Unionists. Whether that larger entity be Britain or Ireland does not in theory matter so much; I think the latter alternative would be more likely to provide a lasting solution, if it could but be attained; but of that I see no prospect while the Protestant community holds to its present convictions. My hope, then, is that Britain may be willing to persevere with direct rule from Westminster. I do not at all share the view that the system is inefficient, unresponsive, remote, and undemocratic. Those criticisms for the most part come from local politicians with axes of their own to grind, and with ambitions to recover power for themselves. It is cumbersome, there is under-representation in the Westminster parliament, and there has been (in my judgement) a falling-off of efficiency at the lower levels of Civil Service administration. But Ulster has good cause to be grateful to successive Secretaries of State and their ministers, both Labour and Conservative. Some mistakes have been made, of course: but on the whole Ulster has received fair, honest, impartial, diligent, and efficient government such as it never received in the days of Stormont: and I have been close enough to the workings of both systems to advance that opinion with confidence.

*   *   *   *

I do not advocate direct rule as the permanent and unalterable answer to the problem. The draftsman of the Act of Union of 1800 inserted the words 'for ever'; that is not a mistake to be made twice. I should dearly like to envisage some kind of reunification of the two parts of Ireland, and at the same time some reunification between Ireland and Scotland, Wales, and England; perhaps through some federal link, perhaps as a part of the drawing-together of Europe. At present, that is a political impossibility. But who can tell what may not happen in a century's time, or two centuries? Who can tell what consequences may flow from the movements for Scottish and Welsh independence? Or how the European Common Market may develop?

Of one thing I am certain: there is unlikely to be any amicable resolution of the Ulster problem in my lifetime; probably not in that of my children. The wounds of the last ten years are too deep. The children of those who have been murdered or maimed, the children of those who have murdered and maimed others, will not themselves forget, and will not allow others to forget, the terrible wrongs that have been suffered and inflicted in these Troubles.

But there is a pattern in history, and certainly a pattern in the history of Ulster. There will come a time when the fires of passion and grievance will burn lower, when once again an impatient generation will genuinely wish to put an end to the divisions of three centuries and more. Such a moment of equilibrium occurred in Ulster in the late 1780s; had the leaders of the United Irishmen been willing then to bring together Protestant and Catholic for peaceful purposes, not for an armed (and doomed) rebellion, much might have been achieved. Another such moment perhaps occurred during the 1830s, between the passing of Catholic Emancipation and the Famine, despite the unrest of that period. Yet another such period came in the late 1860s, the time of my great-grandfather's enthusiastic involvement in the politics of liberalism and reform. And, in my own lifetime, such an opportunity certainly existed in the middle 1960s. What a lost opportunity that was! For the first time in a century the Catholic community in Ulster expressed willingness to forget old scores and to play a constructive part in public affairs. Had the Protestant majority been ready to respond with even a modicum of generosity, the Troubles need never have happened. And it would, then, have taken little enough to satisfy legitimate Catholic complaints; had the Unionists then conceded voluntarily only a fraction of what they have since conceded under the duress of British and world opinion, they might have retained, with some honour, their constitution, their parliament, their government, and their leadership. But all of these, including honour, the Protestants of Ulster have needlessly thrown away.

I am being wise after the event. I tried my hardest to be wise before the event, but I was not wise enough. I have tried to learn from the experiences of my own lifetime, too late myself to put the lesson into practice. I have tried also to learn from the footnotes of history in which I and my forebears have been involved. If this book serves no useful purpose in my lifetime (which yet I hope it may) it may serve as a heartfelt warning to my children, my remoter descendants, the people then of Ulster – Catholic, Protestant, or neither – to grasp, when next it comes, the opportunity for reconciliation with that warmth and generosity which my own generation lacked.

*   *   *   *

From the windows of the room in which I am writing, I look due south across the three-mile width of Belfast Lough to the little town of Holywood. There I was born, there my great-grandfather lies buried, there I shall no doubt in due season be buried myself. It is an ancient town, though there is not much sign of its antiquity today. King John spent the night there in 1210, and left a tip of 60 shillings for the sailors of a ship from Bayonne that had ferried him over the Lough from Carrickfergus. The Franciscan Monastery, which stood in the holy wood, was burned down in 1572 by the O'Neill of Clannaboy lest it furnish a refuge to Thomas Smith's expedition, of which Lieutenant Jerome Brett was a member. The big ships slide past here now, a mile and a half from my window, on their way in and out of Belfast docks.

To the east, I can see the mouth of the Lough, and beyond, on clear days, the hills of the Mull of Galloway: the nearest point of Scotland is less than thirty miles from my window. On the southern shore of the Lough is Bangor Bay. From the great monastery here, St Colombanus and his twelve companions set out in 575 as missionaries to Gaul, Germany, and Switzerland. Into this bay, in 882, the Viking long-ships slid, burning, plundering, and murdering. In the old castle of Bangor my great-great-great-grandfather Charles Brett was born in 1758; and from Bangor quay he set out for Bordeaux, in hot pursuit of a colleague who had swindled him, in 1790. As a schoolboy, I watched the American fleet assemble there in preparation for the Normandy landings of 1944.

Closer at hand, on the northern shore of the Lough, is the grey bulk of Carrickfergus Castle, built by John de Courcy in the 1180s; besieged and captured by King John in 1210; besieged and captured by Edward Bruce in 1316; besieged and captured in 1760 by Thurot with his three

French frigates. At Carrickfergus quay William III landed in 1690. Here the poet Louis MacNeice spent his childhood. The enormous chimney of the power station at Kilroot, towering over the town, stands almost on the site of the thatched house in which Jonathan Swift lived for a year in 1695.

To the south-west, beyond Sydenham airport, lie the Castlereagh hills, in a fold of which still stands Charleville, the family home of Charles Brett for fifty years at the turn of the eighteenth and nineteenth centuries. Beyond lie the steeper slopes of Slieve Croob, where many of the rebels took refuge after the battle of Ballynahinch in 1798; and, further again, visible only on clear days, the Mountains of Mourne — some forty miles away — looking down on the barony of Lecale, where my family struck its roots in Ulster three centuries ago.

At the head of the Lough lies Belfast, its skyline dominated by the Goliath cranes of the shipyard; the bulk of a supertanker fitting out; the slim flame-tipped chimney of the oil refinery; the smoke-tipped chimneys of mills, factories, and chemical works. Just visible from my window too is the Cave Hill, its escarpment overhanging the city. The notch at the summit is Mac Art's Fort, an ancient though waterless fortification. Here Henry Joy McCracken sought refuge in 1798 after the battle of Antrim, and watched, vainly, for a ship to take him to America.

I belong to all I see from my window: and, in the same sense, it belongs to me. Has any republican the right to take from me my share in this heritage of Ulster? Has any loyalist the right to take from me my share in this heritage of Ireland?

January–June 1977.

SOURCES AND ACKNOWLEDGEMENTS

This book is intended for the general reader, not the specialist, so I have not thought it appropriate to burden it with the apparatus of notes and bibliography. I have, however, deposited endnoted copies in the Public Record Office of Northern Ireland, in the Linenhall Library, Belfast, in the British Library, London, and in the National Library of Ireland, Dublin.

Most of the material about members of the Brett family is derived from letters, papers, and copies that have either been passed on from generation to generation, or have been preserved in the archives of the family firm. The Public Record Office of Northern Ireland has calendared these, which may be consulted there under reference D 3303. A great deal was unfortunately destroyed in the accidental fire at my great-grandfather's home in 1892. Though I have photographs of most members of the family from about 1850 on, there are few earlier portraits or miniatures that can be identified with certainty. A rather random collection of silver, furniture, china, and curios has survived in the family, but again, few pieces can be attributed with certainty to any specific source — apart from inscribed family bibles and other books.

I have made extensive use of the excellent collections in the Public Record Office of Northern Ireland, and my thanks are due to all its staff, and especially to Brian Trainor, Anthony Malcolmson, and Miss Gertrude Hamilton. The Ward family papers, the Downshire papers, and the Drennan letters proved particularly rewarding. A few of the Brett letters of the eighteenth century, in the Ward collection, were printed in John Stevenson's *Two Centuries of Life in Down,* published in 1920. A number of significant pieces of information, especially about the earliest William Brett, have been culled from the Ormonde papers, and the Calendars of State Papers. The Reynell collection in the Church of Ireland Diocesan Library, Belfast, proved useful. The invaluable collection of Irish material in the Linenhall Library, Belfast, provided an inexhaustible source of printed matter, including Irish newspapers back to the mid eighteenth century; I owe special thanks to the Librarian, James Vitty, and to his staff. Indeed, the mere survival of so admirable an institution — founded in 1788, and now, as then, a symbol of enlightenment in Ulster – has provided heartening encouragement in discouraging times.

Attempts at research amongst the Irish records in Dublin proved more disappointing. The papers relating to the legal profession in the King's Inns have yet to be calendared and indexed. I could not spare the time that would have been needed to undertake extensive research amongst the former Dublin Castle records. Almost all the papers relating to the seventeenth-century settlement of Ulster, and military matters during that period, as well as wills, probate records, and deeds, were destroyed on 30 June 1922, when the Four Courts were fired and land-mines set off in the greatest disaster of the Civil War. Winston Churchill commented at the time 'better a State without archives than archives without a State'. How much better to have had both archives and a State!

For the period of my own lifetime, I am grateful for his help to Sam Napier, with whom I shared twenty enjoyable years of collaboration and friendship. Although I kept most of my Labour Party papers of those years, and used them on occasions, their bulk is daunting, and I made considerable use (which I acknowledge with gratitude) of the unpublished M.Sc. thesis on 'The consensus-forming strategy of the Northern Ireland Labour Party, 1949–1968', by J. A. V. Graham, in the Library of the Queen's University of Belfast.

I have received help, advice, information, and assistance from very many other people, too numerous to mention here; my thanks are due to all of them. It would be both ungrateful and unfilial to end without expressing my very special thanks – and not only for help with this book – to my father.

INDEX